The INFP Book

The perks, challenges, and self-discovery of an INFP

By: Catherine Chea

To all the healers and dreamers: Thank you for filling this world with inspiration, imagination, and compassion.

CONTENTS

Part III

The career path of an INFP

Part IV

INFP and inspiration

Introduction

I wrote this book because I know how challenging life can be when you feel misunderstood most of the time. As an INFP, I've always felt different from the rest of society. INFPs are described as being reserved, imaginative, passionate, creative, and quirky. These are some of the many qualities that make us unique, but also estranged from the rest of the world which often demands for us to be far more extroverted, conventional, and pragmatic than we naturally are. At times, I even feel as if I am not made for an "ordinary" life.

After discovering my personality type and learning more about what it entails to be an INFP, I've felt more understood than ever before. It's relieving to know that there are other people out there who share similar feelings and can relate to my experiences. I now have a better understanding of my motivations and feelings. Learning more about myself has helped me better respond to situations, communicate with others, and ultimately feel more comfortable in my own shoes.

This book will give you a deeper insight to the INFP personality type. You'll learn the common challenges that many INFPs face and ways to overcome them, to become a healthier and more well-rounded individual. I'll share with you my research into my personality type, some personal reflections, anecdotes, and the lessons that I've learned. In doing so, I hope to inspire and connect with other INFPs who might feel lost in this world.

The first part of this book will provide a detailed description of this personality type and look into its cognitive functions and how it manifests in our experiences. The second part dives deep into my personal struggles and how it relates to my personality. I will also look at some tools that I've developed to help me cope with different situations. The third part focuses on how I discovered my career (I know many INFPs struggle in this department, so it deserves an entire section), and the last part features inspirational tidbits to further show how INFPs can truly shine.

And finally, although I'm writing this book for INFPs, it's not exclusive to people who identify as this personality type. This book is for anyone who is interested in learning about the perks, challenges, and self-discovery of being an Introverted, Intuitive, Feeling, and Perceiving (INFP) personality type.

INFPs can be an unstoppable force who can move mountains—not just in their dreams, but in the real world. And this book will show you how this can be done.

Part I

A portrait of the INFP

"Even now, when I see my name on paper, I feel that the world is intruding unduly on my privacy. I ought to be anonymous."
– *A.A. Milne*

Chapter 1.

What's an INFP?

*"I know that I am what I am, but I am not sure what I am." – **Mason Cooley***

If you're reading this book, you might already have an idea of what an INFP is—being one of the sixteen personality types in the Myers-Briggs Type Indicator (MBTI). This personality assessment was constructed by Katherine Briggs and her daughter Isabel Myers Briggs and is based on the typological theory proposed by Carl Jung.

The purpose of the MBTI is not to put you in a box, but to help you with your self-discovery by understanding the lens through which you see the world. Unfortunately, due to the popularity of this test, there is a vast internet-based culture surrounding it that has created many misleading generalizations. There are blogs, free tests, YouTube videos, celebrity types, and memes about MBTI all over the internet!

Many of these resources describe the personality types based on their common characteristics and observed behaviors, without referring to the cognitive functions in Jung's typology. This leads to stereotypes and even encourages a biased self-assessment (since it may sound more appealing to be a Thinker than a Feeler).

However, the truth is, each personality type is multifaceted and embodies all of the cognitive functions in Jung's typology in varying degrees. Your four letter code, which designates you as one of the sixteen personality types, does not restrict you to only four cognitive preferences. For instance, although an INFP stands for *Introversion, Intuition, Feeling, and Perceiving*, this does not mean that INFPs always prefer introversion over extroversion, or that we don't make decisions based on logic. But before I get too ahead of myself, I will first explain the main dichotomies in the MBTI, and then I'll proceed to clarify the functions.

The dichotomies

The cognitive preferences can be understood in pairs of opposites:

Introversion vs. Extroversion
Sensing vs. Intuition
Thinking vs. Feeling
Judging vs. Perceiving

Combining the four individual preferences yields sixteen distinct types of personality, which are represented by each of its letters.

The first letter

"E" stands for Extroversion and "I" stands for Introversion. This designates where you prefer to get your energy from: the outer world or the inner world. People who prefer Extroversion are energized by interacting with their external environment; they feel the need to surround themselves with people, things, or activities that will help them recharge. People who prefer Introversion orient their energies to their inner world and recharge by giving themselves alone-time to think and reflect.

The second letter

"S" stands for Sensing and "N" stands for Intuition. These are perceiving functions, which identify how a person typically gathers information. People who prefer Sensing prefer to acquire concrete information from their immediate environment. They are considered pragmatic and like to look at facts first and then form an idea. In contrast, people who prefer Intuition are more conceptual and prefer to gather information by focusing on patterns, meanings, and future possibilities. Instead of learning through hands-on experience, they prefer to learn by thinking through a problem and like to see the big picture instead of facts. They often like to look at possibilities without ever implementing them.

The third letter

"T" stands for Thinking and "F" stands for Feeling. These are judging functions, which identify how a person makes decisions in the world. People who prefer Thinking tend to make decisions or reach conclusions by focusing on non-personal logical analysis. People who prefer to make their decisions through Feeling tend to concentrate on people-centered values. Although Feelers are motivated by a subjective outcome, such as considering how their choices would affect another person's well-being, this does not mean that they are irrational; rather, they focus on subjective values more than Thinkers.

The fourth letter

"J" stands for Judging and "P" stands for Perceiving. This letter identifies whether the person takes a Judging or Perceiving attitude towards the outer world. People who prefer a Judging attitude like to make decisions and reach closure; they function best when there is structure and order in their daily lives. People who prefer a Perceiving attitude enjoy gathering as much information about the outer world as possible; they tend to function best when they can take a flexible, adaptable, and spontaneous approach to the world.

Thus:

- E or I refer to a person's preferred energy flow

- S or N refer to a person's preferred form of perception
- T or F refer to a person's preferred form of judgment
- J or P refer to a person's preferred attitude towards the external world

The cognitive functions

Going beyond the four letters

Many personality assessments test your preferences from a spectrum, such as whether you prefer introversion or extroversion. The results that you're given show you which dichotomies (I/E, S/N, T/F, J/P) you lean towards. However, such tests leave a lot of room for inconsistency. People may have different answers depending on the context of the question and their mood or thought process at the time. For instance, although I am a Perceiver, I also have a Judging attitude towards the world when it comes to certain things. For this reason, I was mistyped as an INTJ and an INFJ when I took the online MBTI assessments.

The most accurate way to determine your MBTI personality type is to understand the dynamics of Jung's typology. This is commonly overlooked by people who are new to the Myers-Briggs Type Indicator. Looking at the origins of MBTI, Jung's typology, gives you a more insightful and holistic account of the various personalities. Doing so involves examining the role of each function.

The cognitive preferences can be broken down into eight distinct functions. Each function carries an orientation towards the inner world or the outer world, which is represented by a lower case "i" for introversion or "e" for extroversion. Each of the functions can be understood as either a judging function (which is concerned with decision making) or a perceiving function (which is concerned with gathering information). Below is an overview of the eight cognitive functions. I've also assigned characters to each one for visualization.

Perceiving Functions (S/N)	
Extroverted Sensing (Se)	— Gathers information from the immediate context in the physical world — It's the **keen observer** that notices things in its environment and recognizes "what is"
Introverted Sensing (Si)	— Reviews past experiences and archives information — It's the **archiver** that says, "Remember the time when…"
Extroverted Intuition (Ne)	— Searches for patterns and possibilities by interpreting situations and relationships from external data

	— It's the **idea generator** that likes to ask, "What could be?"
Introverted Intuition (Ni)	— Draws conclusions and foresees implications, reaching an inner understanding of the world — It's the **forecaster** that makes statements about "what will be."

Judging Functions (T/F)	
Extroverted Thinking (Te)	— Organizes and systematizes for efficiency — Achieves objective goals by setting parameters and checking for consequences — It's the **commander in chief** that says, "This is how it's done."
Introverted Thinking (Ti)	— Analyzes and evaluates principles with the goal of understanding a framework or model — It's the **engineer** that wants to understand how systems work

Extroverted Feeling (Fe)	— Seeks harmony within a group, focusing on the values and feelings of others — It's the **human resources department** which tries to ensure that everyone is happy
Introverted Feeling (Fi)	— Preserves personal values and serves as a moral compass — It's the **artist** that makes itself known through self-expression

Each of the sixteen personality types in the MBTI embody all of the eight cognitive functions. What sets each of them apart is the order in which we use them. The dynamics of Jung's typology can be understood as a hierarchy of consciousness. The primary functions are higher in the stack and are more accessible to the consciousness, whereas the shadow functions are lower in the stack and lie deeper within the unconscious.

Because each personality type has a unique functional stack, it's impossible to be more than one type. As well, your personality type does not change over time. If you find that you change your cognitive preferences from time to time, it's either because your shadows are at work or you're jumping the stack, in which your functional stack is not operating in a natural top-down fashion.

The INFP's functions

The order of the cognitive functions for INFPs are as follows:

The primary functions

Introverted Feeling (Fi)
Extroverted Intuition (Ne)
Introverted Sensing (Si)
Extroverted Thinking (Te)

The shadow functions

Extroverted Feeling (Fe)
Introverted Intuition (Ni)
Extroverted Sensing (Se)
Introverted Thinking (Ti)

You can also envision your functional stack as an iceberg. Your primary functions are visible on the surface of the ocean, whereas your shadows are hidden beneath. The iceberg's surface, your dominant function, is supported by layers beneath it: your auxiliary (second function), tertiary (third function) and inferior (fourth function) which lie within your subconscious.

Although each of the sixteen personality types shares the same functions, they manifest themselves differently depending on which dominant function they support. Each personality's iceberg has a different appearance and structure even though they share the same elements. For instance, Extroverted

Intuition would serve a different purpose for an INFP than an INTP. An INTP would use Extroverted Intuition to help them explore logical possibilities. In this way, they can better understand an objective framework, whereas an INFP would use Extroverted Intuition to look at different perspectives to explore their personal values and feelings.

Here's a further explanation of the primary functions of an INFP.

Dominant function: Introverted Feeling (Fi)

For an INFP, Introverted Feeling is the primary driver. Because of this, we strive to be authentic and stay true to our values. Every decision we make is a reflection of who we are and what we believe in. We often need to reflect and express our inner-most thoughts and feelings to recharge. When you care deeply about the inner life of another, feel compelled to fight for a cause you believe in, or are making moral judgments about what's right and wrong, you're using Fi.

Auxiliary Function: Extroverted Intuition (Ne)

This function complements our dominant function in two ways: 1) It's a perceiving function that balances out our Fi, which is a judging function 2) Its energy flow is extroverted, which is the opposite of the energy flow of Fi. Extroverted Intuition is what feeds our Introverted Feeling with new information, entertaining different possibilities and helping us with our quest for meaning. When you're trying to learn more about the world and yourself through exploring cultures, reading a book or engaging in dialogue, you're using Ne.

Tertiary function: Introverted Sensing (Si)

The tertiary function is the opposite of the auxiliary function. In our case, Introverted Sensing (Si) is the opposite of Extroverted Intuition (Ne). While Ne is busy looking at patterns and possibilities, Si is storing impressions from our experiences in the memory lane. If you find yourself feeling nostalgic and reminiscing in the past, you're using Si.

Inferior function: Extroverted Thinking (Te)

Our Extroverted Thinking (Te) is the polar opposite of our dominant Fi function. It helps us look at things practically and tries to keep us organized. Because it's an inferior function, we'll burn out quickly if we rely on it too much. It can also be triggered in an unhealthy manner while under stress. When you're trying to get things done in a practical way, such as organizing your work environment, or when you're applying logic to help you solve problems in science and mathematics, you're using Te.

The shadow side of an INFP

In *Gifts Differing*, Isabel Briggs Myers explains that everyone has a shadow side. She says, "Just as the conscious personality is the product of the best-developed processes, the shadow is the result of the least-developed part, which a person rejects and disowns." The shadow is described to use relatively simple and primitive kinds of judgment and perception, not intentionally in the service of conscious aims and often acts in defiance of conscious standards. If a person were to behave outside of their usual standards, it's likely that their shadow is at work.

Naomi Quenk explains that in Jung's system, the shadow is an archetype and that "includes those things people are unable or unwilling to acknowledge about themselves, such as undesirable character traits, weaknesses, fear and lapses in morality, or desirable qualities such as intelligence, attractiveness, and leadership skills. The shadow is a key component of a person's personal unconscious, a layer of the psyche that is more accessible than its much larger counterpart, the collective unconscious."

According to Jung, the route to the unconscious mind happens through the inferior function. In the case of INFPs, this is Extroverted Thinking. When an INFP becomes anxious or stressed, our shadows will manifest through our Te, causing us to become overly critical, bitter and judgmental. For example, let's say an INFP is offended by someone after being criticized by them. An INFP might respond by finding flaws in their arguments and picking at their errors in a heated debate. However, since many INFPs shy away from conflict, we might choose the passive aggressive route by making indirect remarks or suggestions such as "Have you not…?" to pick on someone's shortcomings or "mistakes."

INFPs can return to equilibrium by regaining control over our Introverted Feeling, which may include the need to find a healthy outlet to express our feelings, having our feelings validated, and allowing the situation to transpire on its own. INFPs in general have a love–hate relationship with our inferior function; at times, it can be very helpful, and at times it can bring out the worst in us. This relationship will continue to appear throughout different parts of this book.

I won't discuss the shadow functions at length, as there are contending theories. I also don't find it crucial to understanding the personality types—only that it's interesting to note that we use all eight functions, but four of them lie within the unconscious realm and may show up unexpectedly. As well, Jung's typology didn't assign a functional stack for our shadows, so I'll leave it at that. Although, an interesting theory suggests that each of the shadow functions correspond to one of our primary functions as its unconscious pairing. Another theory about shadows is that it manifests as the reversal of our four primary stacking, so instead of using Fi-Ne-Si-Te in this order, under stress INFPs use Te-Si-Ne-Fi and would resemble a premature ESTJ.

Moving on, having explained all of the functions of an INFP, all of the important characters in this book have been introduced! As you turn the pages, you'll familiarize yourself even more with these characters and develop a further understanding of the INFP personality type.

Chapter 2.

What it's like to be an INFP

The functional makeup of an INFP comes with a variety of unusual traits and experiences. This chapter is a compilation of a variety of things that INFPs can relate to, based on my reflections and observations. Let's begin with some of the things that make INFPs look like a walking paradox.

A walking paradox

You might notice that although INFPs are perceiving types, who prefer an adaptable lifestyle, we lead with a judging function, Introverted Feeling, which is concerned with establishing order. Why is this? Because our feelings are introverted, we conduct our external lives mainly through our auxiliary, Extroverted Intuition. This allows us to be open-minded, flexible and adaptable—until our core values are being violated, then we stop adapting.

It's not uncommon for INFPs to have strong beliefs and opinions and yet be indecisive when it comes to making everyday choices. This is just one of the many paradoxes of having an INFP personality type. Here are more contradicting things about INFPs:

We want to help others, yet we resist human contact

INFPs are true idealists who want to make the world a better and more compassionate place. We are highly empathetic individuals who have the capacity for deep caring. Although we are very interested in helping others, we can also be extremely reserved and private. As introverts, we need a lot of alone time to recharge, as social interactions can be draining.

We're both curious and shy

INFPs enjoy the exploration of new ideas and possibilities. We are very curious when it comes to learning about the world, and that includes learning about human nature and different cultures. At the same time, we can be shy and hesitant to open ourselves to people who we aren't familiar with. This is because we are conscientious, need time to reflect, and do not like to engage in shallow conversations. We take our encounters quite personally and are highly sensitive, so we may be wary of letting just anyone into our lives.

INFPs can be extremely determined or apathetic

We seem to run on an on-off switch. We can either be extremely obsessive about something or completely indifferent. That's because Fi is our primary driver, so we are motivated by what feels right. If we come across something that excites us, we can become extremely passionate, even neglecting basic needs such as sleep in the pursuit. Conversely, it can be tough for us to find any motivation to finish a task or partake in a discussion if it doesn't spark our interest.

We can be easygoing or stubborn

INFPs are easygoing and flexible, especially when it comes to making everyday decisions. We also like to entertain different ideas and possibilities, thanks to our auxiliary Ne function, and are open to looking at things from many perspectives. However, we have strong personal values due to our Fi and are reluctant to compromise them. We stand our ground and do not easily surrender in the face of adversity. For instance, as an INFP, I believe in staying true to myself, so I often resist giving up my individuality and values to conform, be part of a clique, and please others. INFPs might get bullied for choosing to be a square peg in a round hole, but we wouldn't have it any other way.

INFPs are perfectionists but can also be negligent

We hold high standards for ourselves and can be perfectionists. For instance, we might re-read an email several times before hitting send.

At the same time, as Intuitives, we prefer to focus on the big picture rather than spend time working out the details of something. Likewise, sometimes we get lost in our idealism and neglect more practical matters.

We're unconventional and quirky, but also traditional

INFPs are highly individualistic people who break free from the status quo. We choose our unique pathway rather than doing what society expects of us. At the same time, we can be traditional due to our high values and sense of nostalgia. We are extremely loyal and have clear beliefs about right and wrong. We also attach meaning to things from the past because of our Introverted Sensing function, so it's not unusual for INFPs to hold onto childhood toys, treasured collections, or family memorabilia.

We want to be autonomous and free but also have stability and order

INFPs value autonomy and prefer to do things freely without any impediments. We like to be creative, expressive and explore new things without being burdened by repetitive tasks and strict orders. At the same time, we are drawn to our inferior Extroverted Thinking function and desire some stability and structure in our lives—or else things may get a little too chaotic. We may find our lives to be quite disorganized when we are being carried away by our imagination; we need something to ground us in reality.

We feel happy and sad at the same time

INFPs feel deeply and can experience a full breadth of emotions. We can vividly recreate experiences and feelings through our imagination. We may even experience several emotions simultaneously, such as feeling both pleasant and melancholy.

We want the ideal partner, but may find ourselves drawn to toxic relationships

When it comes to relationships, we may find ourselves falling into one of two traps: We struggle to find our Cinderella or Prince Charming, or end up in a toxic relationship. Because we are highly idealistic, we may have unrealistic expectations when it comes to dating. At the same time, we are crusaders who want to save others. In doing so, we may end up in an unhealthy relationship, attracting narcissists and other toxic individuals who take advantage of our unconditional empathy.

INFPs are both children and old souls

INFPs can sometimes seem childlike because we tend to be optimistic and can see life through rose-colored glasses. In spite of our whimsical and free-spirited nature, we are also old souls: we experience emotions intensely, have high levels of empathy and can see many possibilities in a given situation. With these gifts come incredible insight, depth, and wisdom.

Other INFP experiences

In addition to feeling like a walking paradox, here are other experiences that invariably make INFPs feel like a different species altogether.

Seeing fake people everywhere

Or at least that's how it seems. Because Introverted Feeling is our dominant function, we value authenticity. This translates to us wanting people to be their true selves, even in public. So when people mask their true feelings or say or do things just to conform, we feel like hurling. We see through people's fake happy smiles, and we're irritated by show-offs and superficiality. We have high levels of empathy and can often quickly recognize how other people are feeling, so other people end up venting to us and relying on us for emotional support. The rest of the world is led to believe that they're living the perfect life, but we've heard all their problems, so we know the truth. Hence, we start seeing fake people everywhere.

Spending half of our time daydreaming

INFPs have a direct relationship with our inner world: We explore our innermost passions and values (our Fi) through our auxiliary function, Extroverted Intuition; our tertiary function, Introverted Sensing, then archives this inner exploration in the form of memories and dreams. This enables us to have a vivid and detailed recollection of our imagination.

As a result, we usually find ourselves living in two worlds: our imagination, and the world of reality. Sometimes, we feel like characters from a fantasy or sci-fi novel who can travel through portals into different realms. We often zone out, imagining ourselves living a different life and seeing how things could be in the future, and then returning to the real world, which looks so much blander in comparison.

Becoming obsessed with people or projects

When INFPs care about something, we care about it deeply, to the point that we are afraid of appearing over-the-top hysterical about it to friends and family. For example, we might become obsessed with someone else's life and problems, giving quite a bit of thought to the things that would make them happy and be overly concerned with how they're feeling throughout the day. And when it comes to an idea or a project that sparks our interest, we might become extremely devoted to it, allowing it to take over our thoughts.

Feeling anything but "normal"

We might give off the vibe that we're perfectly normal people who live ordinary lives. But that's only how we look outwardly. Inwardly, we live a life of adventure, imagination, and emotion. But most people don't see this because as introverts, we're typically private and reserved. We're like a raging sea within a rain drop.

Hating to have to pay attention to everyday necessities

When it comes to day-to-day tasks, such as doing chores, paying bills and even combing our hair, we'd rather not have to deal with these things (hence I keep my hair short), so we can have more time to focus on the big picture. Some days, I wish there was a food pill so I wouldn't have to worry about groceries or where to eat. It would be even nicer to have my own robot who could vacuum and do my accounting. Because we are so focused on the big picture, we are often oblivious to the details of our surroundings; such as a stain on the carpet or if a tree near our lawn goes missing (yes, this did really happen to me—a big tree was cut down by the city workers and I didn't even notice).

Having high moral values, even if we're not religious

Many INFPs are religious, but others are not. Whatever our spiritual beliefs are, at times we may feel like a walking bible. We can be judgmental of people if they break our moral codes on honesty and integrity. We also hold ourselves to a high standard, and when we violate our code, we may obsess over our failure, even long after everyone else has forgotten. For instance, I've mentally beaten myself up for hours after I said something that might have offended someone.

Communicating our thoughts and ideas well in writing, but struggling to articulate them verbally

Many INFPs are gifted in writing. We love playing with language and ideas and using our writing to explore the human condition. But even when we're not working on our novel or composing a poem, we still prefer to write our thoughts rather than speak them. Meaning, we'll likely send you a text or an email, instead of calling you on the phone. In fact, we often struggle to articulate our thoughts in the moment, when talking with someone. This is because we need plenty of time to process information and reflect on how something resonates with our inner values. For instance, because I think so much and don't know where to begin, I often feel as though I am speaking gibberish when talking to people; this makes me more anxious, especially if I don't have the patience to try to figure out what I mean.

Having too many ideas and aspiring to be many things

Thanks to our strong Extroverted Intuition, we never seem to run out of ideas, and we're always fascinated by new things. If I had to count all the business cards that I've had, it would be at least ten; I've had so many different career aspirations, from being a biomedical engineer to an interior designer to a lounge pianist! Currently, I work in marketing, and I am always the person proposing tons of content ideas—although my agency can only implement a few. In conversation, I find myself bouncing from one topic to the next, as I discover something else that catches my attention.

It used to frustrate me that I had such a scatter-brained, but now I've come to appreciate that this is my way of exploring new ideas and learning new things.

Not having figured out how to sync with time in the real world

INFPs are always either running late or arriving ridiculously early (in fear of being late). That's because, as Perceivers, we're very casual about time and determining how long it takes to get from point A to B stresses us out. In high school, I always found myself running through the halls to my next class as the William Tell Overture blared from the school speaker, warning students we were almost late.

Finding comfort living within our bubble and relating to the hobbit life

Hobbits—as in Frodo Baggins from *The Lord of the Rings* —and INFPs have a lot in common. We both like to live in the comfort of our homes, tending our gardens, relaxing in the green hills, drinking tea, and creating a shelter from the rest of the world. Just like hobbits, we like warmth and comfort—but also a little adventure now and then, so we have interesting stories to tell our friends.

INFP stereotypes

There are also a lot of misleading stereotypes about the INFP personality type on the Internet. We're thought to be indecisive, emotionally vulnerable and overly idealistic, among other things. I think that's why it took me so long to identify myself as an INFP —not all those stereotypes resonate with me.

Let's shed some light on some of the common misconceptions about this personality type.

INFPs are not logical

Introverted Feeling is the INFP's dominant function. This means we are very in tune with our emotions and internal value system. We naturally base our decisions on what's in line with our core values. But this does not mean we're incapable of logical reasoning. In fact, we can be quite good with reason —especially if our inferior function, Extroverted Thinking, is well developed. For instance, as an INFP, I find myself tapping into my Te at times. I minored in mathematics at university, and I wanted to challenge myself and further develop my left brain. I often find myself using Te to serve further my Fi goals, such as creating logical and sound arguments to defend my views on feminism.

INFPs are crybabies

Without a doubt, INFPs have strong emotions. My emotions can run very deep in such a way that makes me feel like an old soul. However, on the surface,

INFPs more often display a calm and quiet demeanor, because our feeling function is introverted; therefore, our feelings and values are invisible to others, which sometimes makes us a mystery, even to the people who are closest to us. So it's a rare sight to see us display our raw emotions outwardly—and when it does happen, you know it's a big deal. I can only recall a few moments in my life when I've had an emotional outburst in front of someone (and I only let it happen because I trusted that person). It usually happens when I have too much emotion bottled inside, that I can no longer contain.

INFPs are emotionally tortured

INFPs are emotionally sensitive people, but we're also very resilient. Even though we have dark periods, we're quite flexible and adaptable when it comes to dealing with the vicissitudes of life. We have an inner light that prevents us from being too cynical, and we tend to look at life with optimism. As an INFP, I'm very aware of my emotions and am capable of recreating emotions within my imagination. My imagination can also provide a sanctuary from the miseries of the world.

INFPs live in a fantasy world and are indifferent to reality

Okay, I'm not going to lie... it's true that INFPs see things in a way that is rather idealistic (and we're prone to daydreaming), but that doesn't mean that we're always removed from reality.

We are aware of the reality that exists outside of our idealism, in which we are invested in creating a real impact on the world by making a positive difference in the lives of others. We hope to bring forth something insightful and enlightening from our "fantasy world" to the real world. Our idealism enables us to see the best in others, in spite of recognizing their flaws, and we wish to help others realize their potential.

INFPs lack motivation

Motivation is something that depends on the individual and not on the personality type. Although perceiving types such as INFPs struggle with following through (because we have so many ideas), many have also proven to be fruitful and industrious. INFPs are especially motivated when we are passionate about something or when something feels right—and it doesn't have to be anything momentous. It could be something as simple as decorating and cleaning a room after we felt tired of seeing how messy it has become. Or it could be writing a 50-page paper about a topic we're interested in.

Chapter 3.

INFPs and other types

*"Always remember that you are absolutely unique. Just like everyone else." – **Margaret Mead***

Common mistypes

It's quite common for mistypes to happen, especially when you take the assessment for the first time or read a basic description of the personality types without understanding the functions. When I first took the official MBTI assessment, I was mistyped as an INTJ. Having taken the test again online, I mistook myself for an INFJ. Here, I will explain some of the common types that INFPs have been mistyped as (and vice versa), to give a better picture of the unique qualities of an INFP personality type.

INFP or INFJ?

INFPs and INFJs are most often mistyped for one another as we share very similar descriptions. We're both described as complex, misunderstood and emphatic, among other things. Before I understood the cognitive functions, I used to think that I was an INFJ myself. The reason why we are easily confused for one another is that it's difficult to differentiate between the "J" and the "P" types when taking these online assessments. As you're aware, although INFPs are perceiving types, we lead with a judging function, and can be extremely goal orientated and motivated when it comes to accomplishing something that we firmly believe in. However, if you look at the main functions of INFPs and INFJs, we are quite different. Here's a look at the INFP's and INFJ's primary functions:

INFP: Fi-Ne-Si-Te

INFJ: Ni-Fe-Ti-Se

One of the key ways to tell the difference between these two types is that INFPs are more individualistic than INFJs. INFPs are much less comfortable with the notion of giving up our individuality and beliefs to seek harmony. That's because it's important for us to stay true to our values. On the other hand, INFJs are described to be social chameleons because they often compensate their individualism to be accommodating to other people.

As Briggs says in *Gifts Differing*, "The individualism of the INFJs is often less conspicuous not because their inner vision is less clear and compelling, but because they care enough about harmony to try to win acceptance of their purposes." As a result, INFJs may appear to be quite extroverted at times and blend in with their social surroundings, mirroring other people's behaviors to make everyone feel comfortable—which is not usually the case for INFPs.

INFPs are also less concerned about the external world and its complexities than INFJs. The goal of our Introverted Feeling, as Jung describes in *Psychological Types*, is to "seek an image which has no existence in reality, but which it has seen in a kind of vision. It glides unheedingly over all objects that do not fit in with its aim… The depth of this feeling can only be guessed—it can never be precisely grasped."

INFPs are compelled by an intense feeling to seek this inner expression and truth that's invisible on the surface and independent of our external realities. What's most important for INFPs is to feel personally connected to and in tune to whatever decisions we end up making. The decision itself is less important than the fact that it has been made on our terms, since our volition enables us to express who we are. For this reason, we strongly revolt when our personal feelings have been overlooked, as we weren't given a freedom of choice. For instance, INFPs abhor working in an environment that is too rigid or being a part of an organization that has too many rules and protocols. We also strongly dislike being told what's in our best interest because we would rather make this discovery on our own.

In general, we want power and mastery over ourselves, without external impediments and we wish the same for others. For this reason, we tend not to be hungry for political power. As well, we don't usually care what the social norms are or what people "expect" from us; but deep inside, we hold within us an intense set of emotions and inner values that we will not stray from.

On the other hand, INFJs are more intent on understanding the affairs of others. They would even compromise their individuality to fulfill their inner vision and to seek harmony. I'm also not suggesting that INFPs don't have a vision, only that's it's vaguer and more open-ended than that of INFJs'. For instance, I'm a feminist in an ideal sense: I firmly believe that individuals should be valued regardless of their gender, but I'm also less interested in dealing with its political implications since the complexity of reality takes me further away from reaching my inner core.

Another noteworthy difference between INFPs and INFJs is that INFJs absorb emotions, whereas INFPs mirror them. INFJs use Fe to tune into other people's feelings. They even absorb other people's emotional states and experience their feelings as if they were their own. Because INFJs are often so focused on other people's feelings, they may even be oblivious to their own feelings. In contrast, INFPs are very self-aware because of Fi. We can feel other people's emotions by mirroring them within ourselves. When we see a person under distress, we may experience those feelings just as strongly, because they may trigger certain memories that are vividly re-experienced.

INFP or ISFP?

INFPs and ISFPs (Fi-Se-Ni-Te) are quite similar and can be easily mistyped for one another. Both types have a dominant Fi, in which we are highly individualistic and value personal expression. The main difference between INFPs and ISFPs lies within our auxiliary function. INFPs use Extroverted Intuition as our auxiliary, which enables us to pick up on and interpret possible meanings behind external data. As a result, we spend much more time in our head. We like to contemplate big ideas, daydream, think about the future, reflect on our experiences, and may be oblivious to what's going on around us.

On the other hand, ISFPs use Extroverted Sensing, which makes them highly observant of their immediate physical environment. ISFPs prefer to live in the moment. They are very aware of their surroundings and are always finding ways to express themselves in their physical environment, whether it's through art, fashion, or even how they walk. When it comes to the arts, INFPs are fascinated with the meaning, patterns, and symbols, whereas ISFPs have a more realistic attitude towards the world and are less interested in entertaining theoretical concepts.

When it comes to social interactions, INFPs are more self-conscious than ISFPs. INFPs have a tendency to overthink things and see hidden implications and patterns everywhere. We may worry that people misunderstand us and cannot appreciate us for who we truly are, beneath our quiet surface. We also tend to ruminate quite a bit and may get torn up with remorse if we think we've made the wrong decision. In contrast, ISFPs tend to take social interactions at face value, are less self-conscious, and are forward in their approach.

INFP or ENFP?

ENFPs (Ne-Fi-Te-Si) often mistype themselves as INFPs, because they are considered to be one of the most introverted types among the extroverts. They also share similar functions as INFPs, except their dominant and auxiliary are reversed.

ENFPs like to partake in the excitement of the external world, much more than INFPs; they continually seek new ventures and opportunities, hoping to inspire possibility. They are also more outgoing and enjoy the spotlight, whereas INFPs are much more reserved and need time to warm up to people.

As INFPs, we prefer to explore our inner rich caverns, rather than explore the physical world, so that we can be in touch with our true selves. In doing so, we run the risk of losing touch with reality. On the other hand, ENFPs may run the risk of losing touch with their personal feelings, after spending too much time with all their endeavors.

INFP or INTx?

INTx (i.e., INTPs and INTJs) may also mistype for an INFP and vice versa because they are all introverts who like to think conceptually and rationally. When I took the official MBTI, I was first mistyped as an INTJ, since I can be quite logical and goal-oriented at times. Having said this, I also know quite a few people who aren't too sure whether or not they're INFPs or INTPs.

Let's start with INTPs (Ti-Ne-Si-Fe). Similar to INFPs, INTPs also have Ne as their auxiliary function, which they use to explore the outer world. The main difference between INFPs and INTPs is that INTPs have a dominant Ti; they are primarily concerned with making sense of the world, within a logical framework such as understanding how a computer works. On the other hand, INFPs have a dominant Fi, and are primarily concerned with making decisions that align with our personal beliefs and moral framework. For instance, when it comes to making decisions, we're more concerned about what's right than what's most logical. I read somewhere that INFPs and INTPs are similar in a way, yet very different. You can say that we see the same world, but from different angles.

INTPs may also be mistyped for INTJs (Ni-Te-Fi-Se) and vice versa, but these two types are quite different. INTPs are more interested in analyzing a problem and discovering where the solution lies, rather than carrying out their ideas; in contrast, INTJs have Ni as their dominant function and are driven by their inner vision with a focus on realizing their goals. In other words, INTPs are more interested in developing and understanding theories, while INTJs are more driven to put theory into practice; meaning, INTJs want solutions that work.

However, both INTPs and INTJs may find it difficult to be attuned to other people's feelings. In a relationship, this could pose a challenge for us INFPs who need lots of emotional validation. This reminds me of a quote from the INFP-Problems Tumblr page:

> *"Sometimes I just hate logical types, because when I feel upset or lonely and all I want to do is have someone sit down and listen to my rantings, they listen for like four seconds and then give me an unsolicited, unnecessarily logical way to fix my problem. I don't want my 'problem' fixed! I just want to know that I'm heard and loved."*

INFPs often feel misunderstood because we think so differently from other personality types. This leads me to the next section.

The misunderstandings amongst various types

Resentment typically occurs amongst different types when we don't understand the motivations behind cognitive functions. Learning about them could help

us better understand ourseleves and the perspectives
of different personality types. As Carl Jung says,
"Everything that irritates us about others can lead us
to an understanding of ourselves." In this section, I'll
compare the INFP's stronger functions (Fi and Ne)
with its introverted/extroverted counterpart (Fe and
Ni), to show where misunderstandings between
different users may arise.

Introverted Feeling (Fi) vs. Extroverted Feeling (Fe)

We could say that the Introverted Feeling is
individualistic and the Extroverted Feeling is
collective.

Introverted Feeling (Fi)	Extroverted Feeling (Fe)
— "Stay true to yourself" — Fi considers first and foremost what is important to them and their values — Creates and reflects internally on beauty and goodness — Has a strong sense of justice — Values the uniqueness in self and others	— "Have courage and be kind" — Fe is attuned to the values and emotions of its surroundings — Strives for harmony — Sees that a certain amount of individuality should be sacrificed to avoid unnecessary conflicts — Is often altruistic and a bit of a pleaser — Has excellent social skills

– Sees "weird" as a compliment – Values honesty – Feels that things should be done because you want to do them	– Wants to create positive feelings in social situations

Types that use Introverted Feeling	Types that use Extroverted Feeling
Dominant Fi users: **INFP, ISFP** Auxiliary Fi users: **ENFP, ESFP** Tertiary Fi users: ISTJ, INTJ Inferior Fi users: ESTJ, ENTJ	Dominant Fe users: **ESFJ, ENFJ** Auxiliary Fe users: **INFJ, ISFJ** Tertiary Fe users: ESTP, ENTP Inferior Fe users: INTP, ISTP

(Source: Raven-MBTI from Tumblr)

Misunderstandings between Fi users and Fe users

Given the same social scenario, a Fi user and a Fe user would respond differently. For instance, if a friend doesn't like watching comedy, but made this suggestion anyway, an extroverted Feeler would think their friend is making a thoughtful gesture by doing something that they normally don't like. An introverted Feeler, such as an INFP, would be much more reluctant to watch this movie if they knew that their friend didn't like it. This is because introverted

Feelers value people's individuality and personal values, whereas extroverted Feelers value collective harmony in which making such compromises is seen as an act of kindness.

When it comes to criticism, an extroverted Feeler would hear the criticism as a third party and think, "who says that to *someone*?" On the other hand, an introverted Feeler would internalize the criticism, taking it much more personally, and think "does that person think of *me* that way?"

Introverted Feelers may believe that extroverted Feelers are inauthentic people pleasers, whereas extroverted Feelers may think that introverted Feelers are selfish for not being willing to make compromises.

In reality, extroverted Feelers aren't blind conformists without any own values. They are simply sensitive to others and embrace many "social roles." But those roles aren't fake masks that hide the true values of a person; rather, are a part of their "true values."

Additionally, introverted Feelers are far from selfish. We value honesty and prefer to speak our mind, and we encourage others to do so as well. We appreciate others as they are and we mean what we say.

Introverted Intuition (Ni) vs. Extroverted Intuition (Ne)

We could say that Introverted Intuition is conclusive and Extroverted Intuition is open-ended.

Introverted Intuition (Ni)	Extroverted Intuition (Ne)
– Filters out biases and refine perception to arrive at "one truth" – Looks at individual parts to see how it makes up a whole system – Foresees implications – Focuses on one major insight – Is cautious and calculating	– Entertains different ideas and possibilities in turn – Seizes new enterprises and activities – Picks up meanings and interconnections to other contexts – Bounces from idea to idea – Is adventurous and spontaneous
Types that use Introverted Intuition Dominant Ni users: **INFJ, INTJ** Auxiliary Ni users: **ENFJ, ENTJ** Tertiary Ni users: ISTP, ISFP Inferior Ni users: ESTP, ESFP	Types that use Extroverted Intuition Dominant Ne users: **ENFP, ENTP** Auxiliary Ne users: **INFP, INTP** Tertiary Ne users: ESTJ, ESFJ Inferior Ne users: ISTJ, ISFJ

Misunderstandings between Ni users and Ne users

A Ni user might grow frustrated with Ne users for appearing to have a short attention span. They might think Ne users, such as INFPs, are scatter-brained, random, and do not have a clear vision or purpose, whereas a Ne user might see Ni users, such as INTJs and INFJs, as being too rigid for rejecting information once they think they have accurately interpreted something already. For example, an INTJ might be convinced that the Myers-Briggs personality assessment is the most reliable personality model out there, while an INFP may be interested in looking at other models to find further explanations for their personality.

In reality, Ne users are not necessarily scatter-brained but want to look at each possibility in turn, to expand their horizons, whereas Ni users are not necessarily rigid for not seeking out new information; they want to investigate one piece of the puzzle more thoroughly to better understand the entire picture.

Some final thoughts on understanding other personality types

As I have shown in this section, the best way to understand other personality types and their perspectives is by developing a good understanding of the cognitive functions and each type that uses them, with reference to your experiences. So even though you may not share the same primary functions as another personality type, such as an ESTP (whose primary functions are Se, Ti, Fe, Ni), you might be able to relate to their struggles. For instance, you understand challenges an ESTP may have with developing an inferior function or respect the fact that they do not hold onto deeply-held values as you do because Fi is less accessible to them. I've discovered that the more that I learn about other personalities, the more I can appreciate our differences and better bridge the gaps in our understanding of one another.

Chapter 4.

Being friends with an INFP

*"Love all, trust a few, do wrong to none." – **William Shakespeare***

When it comes to being friends with an INFP, it's important to note that we prefer to maintain a small circle of friends because we are very reserved. Below are some more things to know about being friends with an INFP personality type:

We may disappear into our own world for a while

Although we value our friendships and deeply care about the people we love, sometimes we need time to ourselves for days or even months to sort out our feelings and thoughts. When this happens, we are re-evaluating meaning in our lives. There have been many occasions when I was going through some sort of existential crisis and felt the need to disappear in order to rediscover my purpose. This might entail traveling for a bit, or finding myself engrossed in my thoughts (and books) for days. After such experiences, I feel like a different person; I'm more enlightened and I have a fresh outlook on life. Often, my friends don't know about these experiences because I keep them private. But they might notice my rekindled energy and spirit.

An example of a time when I needed solitude came after I graduated from high school. I felt lost and I needed a change of scenery. So I decided to enroll in a university that was far away from home on the other side of the country. I then became preoccupied with my philosophy studies, which I stumbled across by chance. During this time, I was out of touch with my good friends because I was trying to figure out who I was.

We prefer a tiny moment of real connection to hours of polite conversation

INFPs value meaning and depth, so we do not like to engage in shallow conversations, such as gossiping, talking about the mundane and day-to-day, and all of the times that you swiped left on Tinder (with the exception of exciting cases that fall outside the norm). For us, small talk doesn't interest us because it lacks substance and feels superficial. However, that doesn't mean we're serious and need to have deep philosophical conversations constantly. We like to have fun and can be quite quirky and silly. What we really crave is the feeling that we've made a genuine connection with you on a personal level. We want to have a shared experience with you, whether it's through something that we can both laugh or cry about.

We also value our space and don't need to text our friends 24/7 to update them on every aspect of our lives. Maintaining this kind of relationship can wear us out in the long run. We prefer to have fewer but more meaningful interactions than plenty of lower quality ones. The funny thing about us is that although we like to be left alone, we don't want to be alone—we long for intimacy and find it hard to come by.

We get hurt easily but we struggle to articulate it

We care for others deeply and easily become absorbed in other people's worlds. Unfortunately, the reverse isn't always true and we may end up disappointed and hurt when we discover that a relationship is one-sided. We value friendships that are mutual and reciprocal; anything that is one-sided is seen as inauthentic—and we despise anything artificial. For many of us, learning to let go of certain toxic people can be difficult because we are extremely loyal. However, although we do get taken advantage of, this is not always the case. Sometimes we feel like we are ignored by our friends, when in reality, they may be very busy or need some space of their own. When our friends don't respond to our messages, we can take it quite personally and feel left out and alone. So, it's important that we communicate these feelings and establish an understanding in order to maintain healthy relationships.

Sometimes we need to be encouraged to open up

INFPs live in our heads most of the time: we like to daydream and contemplate the meaning of life. When we're deep in our thoughts for too long, we have trouble returning to reality. We also need to experience the outer world and open up to others in order to live authentically. But we may have a hard time doing this because we are shy and introverted, so we do appreciate it when others reach out to us or invite us places. We certainly are not party people, but we do look forward to going out every so often.

We are your biggest supporters and you can trust us with your insecurities

We enjoy listening to you and helping you sort through your feelings. We're good at picking up on people's emotions and energy and understanding how they feel. Because of this, we might be able to help you unravel the root of your troubles. Our idealism combined with our strong beliefs about morality enables us to see the best in you and your potential, even though you may not see it yourself. For example, even though you may feel useless and unworthy, we can see your courage and strength, and we will try to help you realize this. We also understand that people make mistakes, so rarely will we judge you. However, please know that although it brings us great joy to help you heal, sometimes we forget to set our own boundaries and end up becoming drained ourselves by carrying too much emotional baggage. This is when we need time to ourselves.

Part II

The troubles in an INFP's life

"Stars can't shine without darkness" – **unknown**

Chapter 5.

The troubles of our past

*"For people like me, who have
blocked out a chunk of their past,
you wonder if you open that door, if
you walk into that room of your
memories, what will happen? Will it
destroy you or will it make you
stronger?"— **Tim Daly***

It's best to shed some light on the challenges of being
an INFP, including the negative emotions that haunt
us. This way, not only do we get the heavy stuff out
of the way, but covering such material first will lay
the groundwork for understanding the healthy
development of an INFP. I believe that a lot of my
self-discovery and personal development is attributed
to overcoming my demons. So brace yourself for a
very personal and heavy read. I strongly believe that
doing so will also help show how INFPs can shine
through the darkness.

The internal wound of an INFP

I know that life can be hard for an INFP. We feel alienated from the rest of the world. Many of us have also been severely hurt in the past, which has led to our need to escape into our fantasies. This prolonged escapism may have caused us to become more isolated from the world, where we then become very lonely and miserable in our sufferings. There are perks to spending time in our inner world as well, but now I'm focusing on the dark side of our personality type.

Beneath our calm demeanor lies very strong emotions, due to our dominant Introverted Feeling function. We can also remember certain things that have happened in our past with great detail, thanks to our tertiary Introverted Sensing function, which archives our memories. Recollections of past hurt and trauma are so deeply felt by us, that they become re-lived experiences. Hearing stories of other people who have experienced similar traumas can trigger a strong emotional reaction within me, even to the point where I find myself sobbing hysterically.

One time I went to a one-week retreat a few hours away from the city in Coburg, Ontario, to gather with around 30 committed change-makers to discuss social injustice and community building. In one of our activities, we sat around in a group therapy setting, where we shared deep personal struggles and oppression that we've each faced. People were exchanging turns, sharing their pains, anxiety, and grief. Some people talked about the abuse that they'd experienced at home, while others shared their struggles with their career or relationships, and some had even contemplated suicide.

The heavy emotions that welled up inside me kept accumulating to the point where I broke down into uncontrollable tears, needing endless supplies of tissue paper. I am usually very well gathered and calm on the surface and don't outwardly display my raw emotions in public. So I even surprised myself with how many emotions I've bottled, which were reflective of my internal wounds. INFPs often hide our emotions from the public because our feelings are introverted and private. When I feel like sobbing, I try to contain my feelings until I find the privacy to let it out with no one watching. However, we sometimes experience emotions that are so intense and overpowering that we can't conceal them so that others may notice our discomfort.

In the past, I've experienced some traumas that became a reoccurring theme throughout my adolescence and early adulthood. These past experiences had been repressed during my childhood and only emerged during my adolescence, where I began to seek counseling services. I won't go into too much detail of my past, as not only am I uncomfortable with sharing everything, I also don't think it's necessary for the purpose of writing this book. I also don't speak on behalf of all INFPs, but from what I've gathered, many INFPs have experienced some ordeal in the past, and so I feel that it's relevant to at least mention it.

As a little background, I had an unconventional childhood. I'm an only child and I've always felt like a loner, even though at times I may appear social. I was separated from my parents when I was three and went to live with my grandparents in Shanghai, China, for a year. This was a time when I was living an entirely different life from the one that I have in Canada. Even though it was so long ago, this was one of the defining moments in my life, where I felt as if I could live in different worlds. I've seen things at an early age where others have not and I have experienced things that were surreal and could have come out of a novel.

My childhood at home, in the suburbs of southern Ontario, Canada was no different, as far as being "ordinary" goes: My disconcerting family dynamics had left me feeling estranged and isolated from the rest of the world. I think this is why I have become a dreamer. I've always found a way to retreat from the miseries of the world, distracting myself in my imaginary world, where I played with toys, read storybooks, and found my creative expression through art and music. And so, even though I had childhood best friends, a part of me had always felt alienated from everyone else.

Seeking help

During high school, I went through my first major breakdown. I overloaded myself with too many courses in one semester—running primarily on my Extroverted Thinking until I completely burned out and crashed. I ended up seeking help from an academic adviser who questioned what I wanted in life. It was at this point when I realized that I was suffering from post-traumatic stress disorder. My hard efforts were a way of hiding from my deeper issues. Being a high achiever in school compensated for the lack of security and stability that I had in my personal life.

I was recommended to seek professional help from a psychologist and this is when I started seeking assistance. It took me a few years and a few counselors and psychologists before I found the right one who was patient and understanding enough to give me the support that I needed. When it comes to getting the right support, it's not easy finding the right person.

Most people aren't counselors and I learned this the hard way. In the past, I tried to open myself up to people who do not understand and even reject my feelings, dismissing them because they are a nuisance. It only makes matters worse when this happens because my feelings are invalidated. I used to feel that people were ignorant and cruel for treating me this way, but I am wiser now, knowing that it's not their fault. Many people are battling with their demons. Not everyone knows how to show compassion and understanding, especially when they are struggling; often, the last thing they want to hear is other people's victimhood because this adds to the burden of their already cumbersome life.

Even those who are certified may not be adept at helping you walk through your psychological process.

Some of them may have too many of their opinions and diagnoses and fail to give you the attention that you deserve. When it comes to seeking counselling, I believe what most people are looking for is someone who is compassionate and makes you feel as if your feelings are heard.

As mentioned in Carl Jung's *Man and his Symbols,* although a psychologist may be able to diagnose a patient's symptom immediately, remedying their problems is a long process; this involves patience and listening until the subject can make their realizations and come to terms with the root problem. Each person is a unique subject and shouldn't be treated objectively as if there is one cure that fits all. I believe that this is the same for INFPs; although we may share the same cognitive functions, no two INFPs are alike, and each of us has our struggles that we must learn how to cope with by ourselves. So hopefully, the experiences that I'm sharing within this book will inspire you to find your path and inner peace.

It's also interesting to note how telling dreams can be about ourselves, our internal struggles and may even foresee our future. Jung's *Man and his Symbols* talks about dreams and their symbols, and the role our unconsciousness play when it comes to understanding ourselves. Your unconscious can often inform you of crucial information about yourself and your motives. For instance, you might have a dream about a plane crash, which may be a metaphor for some aspect of your life that is in danger of ending quickly and unexpectedly.

For myself, I had recurring nightmares from my childhood that continued to persist even while I was at university. I've always had visions of escaping and running away from my ordeal. I was never able to confront that in my real life. So they continued to haunt me even in my dreams, disrupting my sleep. It took me years to eventually turn around from what I was trying to escape from and to stand up for myself. And before I knew it, I no longer had those nightmares and fully recovered from my post-traumatic stress disorder. It's incredible how facing my demons in the unconscious realm had a direct impact on my daily well-being.

I'm very fortunate and thankful for my counselor for giving me the encouragement to master the courage to stand up to my demons. She was very empathetic, asked the right questions, and helped me acknowledge the child that was wrongly hurt in the past, and that none of it was my fault, for I used to take a lot of blame. She helped me realize that no human being, myself included, deserves to feel wounded. However, in the end, it was up to me to make these realizations about myself and to come to terms with my past, to be able to be at peace with it and put it all behind—and most importantly, to stop hating myself and to accept myself as I am.

This is more easily said than done, and I know that traumas don't just go away instantly. It takes a lot of courage, introspection, self-love, forgiveness and patience. I'd like to emphasize the word *patience* throughout this book because I find that myself and other INFPs can be extremely hard on ourselves. This is because of our idealism. Many of the things that we'd wish to accomplish cannot happen within a short time span—and this includes overcoming our demons.

Leaving the past behind

As INFPs, we sometimes find ourselves living our past, in which we try to analyze and make sense of everything that has happened to us. It doesn't necessarily have to be something monumental. It could be an event that has taken place with us recently, and we can't seem to put it to rest. Sometimes I feel like I replay things in my head in a loop: I imagine the scenario again, trying to think of how things could have gone differently, or trying to find meaning and discover who I am by looking backward. A lot of the memories that I replay are usually unpleasant ones, where I hold on to grudges and anger about the injustices that I've experienced.

When this happens, I end up in a dominant-tertiary loop, where I become confined to my inner world instead of rising to new challenges. When INFPs are in this loop, we forgo using our Extroverted Intuition, which gives us new information from our external world. Instead, we skip to our tertiary function, Introverted Sensing, in which we try to understand ourselves by examining memories from our past. In doing so, we lose sight of external possibilities that can help pull us out of the ditch that we have created.

I've spent a chunk of my life analyzing and trying to make sense of my past, hoping that doing so would help me better understand myself and the situation. What usually happens is that I end up digging myself into a deeper hole, instead of digging my way out of it. I end up being stuck in my thoughts and feeling overpowered and impotent.

What helped me let go of the past, and break free from my dominant-tertiary loop, was acknowledging its adverse effect on my present experience. I realized I couldn't continue living this way. My burden held me back from living the life I wanted. I couldn't enjoy the present moment. If you find yourself trapped in your thoughts, realize that you are not bound by your past and that you are free.

One of my favorite philosophy books, *The Ethics of Ambiguity* by Simone de Beauvoir, describes freedom as the necessity to self-consciously choose who one is at every moment. In other words, what has happened to you before, does not have to dictate how you see your life as of this moment; you have freedom to choose how you perceive the world and to think that your past binds you is to deny your own freedom.

On top of this, I didn't want my life to be boring; if I continued to stay in my room and wallow in my miseries and escape into my fantasies, I wouldn't be able to learn and grow and discover interesting things about the world. I wouldn't be able to take action, live authentically, and ultimately find success. Instead, I would be moping around for the rest of my life as a sad, boring, and defeated person. Remaining hurt and victimized will prevent me from doing the things that will make my life interesting. This in itself is a terrifying thought.

When I was finally able to let go of my past, a huge weight was lifted off me. Even so, life still presented its challenges and often I still struggle with negative emotions. But I believe that we face obstacles to become stronger. Each time we are tested, we gain valuable wisdom and insight that help us grow and reach our potential.

It also helps to realize that, in life, pain is inevitable, but suffering is optional. Being happy does not mean to live in the absence of pain, but to enjoy life in spite of it. I believe that happiness doesn't necessarily come easily: It requires work and training our thought process. Over the years, I've developed tools, strategies, and insights that have helped myself and others better manage situations that cause us anxiety, stress, and unhappiness. This will be covered in the next few chapters.

Chapter 6.

Our internal and external conflicts

"The happiness of your life depends
upon the quality of your thoughts:
therefore, guard accordingly, and
take care that you entertain no
notions unsuitable to virtue and
reasonable nature."
— **Marcus Aurelius**

As an INFP, I feel emotions very deeply and intensely. I've often struggled with letting go of the negative emotions that weighed me down. The burdens that I carried were a consequence of the injustices that I've experienced in my personal life. However, I now realize that although others have hurt me, much of the pain I experienced had also been self-imposed.

I know that a lot of INFPs also struggle to handle negative emotions because we take most of our encounters quite personally. Our Introverted Feeling paired with our Extroverted Intuition, continually evaluate and assess our situation, determining how it aligns with our core values. We have a tendency to overthink things and see hidden implications and patterns everywhere and tend to ruminate quite a bit about things that have taken place in our lives. Even though many of our experiences are beyond our control, we often take these matters to heart and see these as reflections of who we are. For this reason, we are highly sensitive individuals who can be easily hurt.

INFPs, in general, dislike aggressive communication and would avoid it all together if possible. If our core values are being threatened, we might respond viciously or shut people out entirely. When we become stressed, anxious, or frustrated, our shadow manifests through our underdeveloped Extroverted Thinking function. When this happens, we are no longer our compassionate and gentle selves; instead, we become bitter, judgmental, and extremely critical of every error we see.

For instance, I remember one time at university when I ended up in a heated argument with a peer about the social implications of polygamy and why it's damaging to women. The position she took violated my core beliefs about justice, which made me extremely infuriated and resentful. We continued arguing our sides to no end, trying to make a logical argument to disprove the contending view, which only escalated the anger that we each felt. The conversation did not end well, damaging our relationship for good.

Because INFPs have deep feelings that are hidden from the surface, others hurt me without even knowing it. I naturally don't take criticism quite well, especially when the comments that are being directed at me are insensitive and demeaning—these can trigger very intense negative emotions. It doesn't make things easier that I'm very conscientious and judge myself quite harshly. So, internalizing other people's criticisms only amplifies the critical voice inside my head.

For instance, one time I tried to explain to a friend that I was experiencing internal turmoil due to my personal circumstances. Instead of getting a compassionate response, I was called out for being "too sensitive, self-pitying, and ungrateful." What makes matters worse is that I often don't communicate how I've been affected by the situation. I keep my hurt to myself. This only exacerbates the pain.

Given my circumstances, I'd prefer to avoid certain people and conflict whenever possible, but sometimes I can't remove the negative people in my life. So I try to mitigate the pain I was experiencing. In doing so, I learned to become more adept at moderating my negative emotions. From my counseling services to reading, I've come across some highly useful methods that have helped me in conflict situations.

Understanding our emotions in relation to the external world

As INFPs, we often feel alienated from the world. This is due to our Introverted Feeling, which gives us our sense of uniqueness and individuality. Our problem isn't that we don't understand ourselves and our feelings; instead, our struggle comes from the notion that others don't understand us. This leaves us feeling misunderstood and isolated. If we don't resolve this issue and it becomes chronic, we can become very cynical and lead a very miserable life.

Although Introverted Feeling enables us to be very attuned with our emotions and values, our sole reliance on Fi would make us suffer—it would push us further away from the external world. When this happens, we tend to be extremely sensitive to criticism and trapped in our thoughts. As idealists, we also become too hard on ourselves and others for not living up to our high standards.

In order to balance out our Introverted Feeling, we have to be open to the external world by using Extroverted Intuition to look at different perspectives, taking in new information, in order to understand the world. Our alienation from the rest of the world occurs when we use Extroverted Intuition in a diminished manner, in which we take in new information only to confirm our subjective biases instead of looking at things for what they are.

A reason why we may find it difficult to look at ourselves from an impersonal standpoint is that we feel that doing so would disregard and reduce our unique experiences, making us common. For instance, it may be hard for us to accept that other people, in fact, are not so much different from us since we all belong to the same humanity. When we disregard our external realities and, essentially, live in our bubble, we prevent ourselves from growing and living authentically.

On the other hand, when we use Extroverted Intuition to its fullest potential, we're be able to look at things with an open mind. When we take in information for the sake of understanding the world around us, rather than taking in information only to support our own ideas, we have a clearer, more objective understanding of the world. This helps us set realistic expectations so that we are not let down by ourselves and others. As well, it also helps us to take criticisms less personally and be more open to constructive feedback.

I understand that it can be challenging to put theory into practice. How can Extroverted Intuition be used to support Introverted Feeling and help dissolve certain negative emotions? Below are some practical tips to help you deal with conflict and manage your feelings.

Create a filter

Realize that you are the ultimate gatekeeper of your emotions. You can choose not to let certain things upset you. As John Green, author of *The Fault in Our Stars* (and fellow INFP), says, "You don't get to choose if you get hurt in this world, but you do have some say in who hurts you." When it comes to dealing with negative emotions that stem from others, sometimes the trick is not to take things personally.

Understand that when people cannot cope with their negative emotions, often they let them out on others. Knowing this has helped me filter negative emotions that have been projected toward me.

Have an emotional checklist

If your negative emotions are bothering you, it helps to go through a checklist. Take a deep breath and try to answer the following questions:

- What am I feeling and what is causing it?
- Is there a way to resolve the situation?
- If not, ask yourself, "Is the problem really a problem in the grand scheme of things?"

Learn about the fundamental techniques of dealing with people

I highly recommend that you read Dale Carnegie's *How to Win Friends and Influence People* if you haven't already. This provides great tips on building people skills, including how to manage conflict. One key point from the book is that the only way to get the best of an argument is to avoid it. Whenever we argue with someone, no matter if we win or lose the argument, we still lose. The other person will either feel humiliated or strengthened and will only seek to bolster their position. We must try to avoid arguments whenever we can.

For instance, let's say someone has made a very controversial post on Facebook about a topic which causes your blood to boil. You begin to casually bring up your point about why their post is problematic, but then don't get the response you were hoping for. Instead, the person rebuttals by making personal attacks on yourself and your character. At this point, continuing to argue with them would only make things worse and would get you nowhere. Nobody likes to admit that their point of view is wrong or flawed because their pride is at stake. Sometimes it's best to keep certain opinions to yourselves. A more compelling way to prove your point is by setting an example, rather than directly arguing with someone.

Find a creative outlet

The thing with emotions is that they cannot be contained. Especially since INFPs bottle up a lot of emotions, they need to be explored and released in some way. When verbal communication has failed, turn to other areas where your emotions can manifest, such as through the arts and music.

The wonders of communicating our feelings through writing

I find that myself and other INFPs have trouble articulating our thoughts and feelings verbally, but we can be quite effective at expressing it through writing. Many INFPs have an aptitude for writing because we are very introspective and we are always looking for meaning in depth. We think quite abstractly and can paint a picture of our feelings through stories and language. Especially for highly sensitive introverts, such as INFPs, communicating our feelings through writing a letter has proven to be highly effective. Often, conflict arises because of miscommunication, and since INFPs' feelings are deeply held and private, it can be a challenge for us to convey them directly—that's why we need to write them down first.

I've learned the value of communicating my feelings through writing when I attended social anxiety workshops provided by my university. Not only has this advice helped me resolve conflicts, but it has also assisted me in assessing and evaluating my emotions. I've gained a newfound confidence in my ability to handle any social situation. Writing also allows me to thoroughly reflect on the situation and express my feelings toward it. It helps bring clarity to the situation as well as enabling me to communicate my perspective more clearly and effectively. Assertive writing has proven to help my friends, myself, and others immensely to resolve a conflict and clarify ambiguities in a relationship.

One time, an instructor told me that I didn't know the subject matter after I asked him a question about my assignment. He told me to go home and read the textbook in a condescending manner, which nearly brought me to tears. I sent an e-mail about how I was feeling with his course and that his refusal to help me had been upsetting. The next day, I received an apology in response. He realized that what he said might have been offensive and offered to provide extra tutorial hours to help his students, including myself. This is a minor case where a letter helped me resolve an issue.

Below are three points to consider when writing a letter to express how you're feeling:

1. Use "I feel" statements

These statements are profound because they phrase the situation so that it reflects your perspective and emotional needs without putting direct blame on the other person. When you frame the letter from your view, rather than presenting a biased narration of the scenario, you avoid attacking the person you're addressing. In doing so, they are less likely to react defensively and more inclined to cooperate with you and understand you.

2. Explain the situation succinctly

It's important to explain the main issues without getting too much into the unnecessary details. The goal of this letter is to get your point across. Writing excessively may come across as off-putting or neurotic, and I find that a paragraph or two is more than sufficient to communicate my thoughts effectively.

3. Be as honest and truthful as possible

Although your letter should be succinct, the most convincing letters are the ones that are incredibly honest. I find this to be the hardest component of writing a letter: writing about your feelings and vulnerabilities to someone so that you and they can better understand how you've been affected by the situation. It takes a lot of courage to do this, but it's worth it in the end. Once you acknowledge your feelings and communicate them, you will find a great weight lifted off your shoulders.

Here's a template for you to try:

Dear _____,

Although it's difficult for me to bring up this subject, I feel that it's necessary to discuss this (conflict/misunderstanding). Because I feel like I can better express myself in writing, I've chosen to write you a letter.

Lately, I've been feeling hurt about (insert situation). When (the situation) happens, I feel as though I (what emotional need is not met).

This has been weighing on me, and I don't want to leave it unresolved. I would appreciate if we can straighten this out soon, but even if we can't I just wanted you to know how I'm feeling.

Sincerely,

You

Even if you do not get a response, simply acknowledging your feelings and knowing that you have done your part to address the situation is often enough to rest your case and improve your outlook. Moreover, when it's written down, you have concrete proof of the exchange. If you don't get a response, not receiving an answer may be an answer in itself.

These tips have proven to be quite effective and have helped a lot of people, including those who have read my Elephant Journal article, *Mindful Communication: 3 Tips for Writing Someone a Letter about How You Feel*. It has been my most read article thus far and has received much praise including this:

"Hi. I love this article. I recently had a family member pass away. I had so much pent up emotions and no way to communicate without hurting others. I had read your article, so I sat down and wrote them a letter. A letter I will never send or show to anyone else. In my grief, I misspoke with someone else, who I'd sent this article to and they wrote me a letter. As someone then receiving the letter, I was able to honestly self-examine my actions and words. The letter didn't insult me or chide me, it simply openly discussed their feelings. Thanks."

It's amazing how powerful written words can be. They give us immediate cathartic release as a channel to address our emotions and needs, in a healthy and constructive manner. They're an effective tool for open communication and prompting concrete solutions to problems we're facing.

Chapter 7.

The problem with self-esteem

"A man who as a physical being is always turned toward the outside, thinking that his happiness lies outside him finally turns inward and discovers that the source is within him." – **Soren Kierkegaard**

Though self-esteem applies to all personality types, I find that many INFPs struggle with this notion because we are so hard on ourselves. Ever since my childhood, I have been self-conscious of my appearance and abilities. There's a cruel voice inside my head that taunts me every so often. It tells me that I'm not good enough and that a part of me is lacking: I could be more accomplished, I could be more outgoing and confident.

In the past, I've worked hard to build my self-esteem: this includes exercising more, achieving higher grades in school, being more positive, and meeting more people. Although these in themselves are admirable goals, I found the pressure to meet my standards overwhelming. One time, I even tried documenting my efforts to stay positive through a series of video blogs, since I was well aware of how negative I can be. Shortly after, however, this plan backfired. I would berate myself whenever I had a bad day. I didn't seem to be significantly happier than what I had been before and I also slightly envied people who seemed more optimistic—all of which made me feel worse.

There were times in my life where I was so down on myself that I felt like a complete failure and ended up in a rut. This often happens when I compare my life to others, thinking that other people are more successful, ambitious, and have a better sense of direction. Doing so only makes me feel even more incompetent. However, I now realize that this helpless feeling is something that I have constructed in my mind. I am somehow able to pave my way out of my despair when I start to look at life from a different angle. When I stop concerning myself with my perceived value, that is my self-esteem, I can begin to pave a more purposeful life and find happiness.

So why has self-esteem failed me?

The problem with self-esteem is that relying on it for our self-worth is like filling a void. This void is insatiable and depends on short-term gratification. At times, when my self-esteem was rising, it was a fleeting moment because it was based on short-lived factors that could not fully quench my ego. My ego wants more self-esteem in order to be enough. It tells me that I should be more confident, prettier, smarter, popular, to be worthy. It doesn't help that as an INFP, I'm extremely idealistic and often don't feel as if I live up to my standards, no matter how hard I try. My focus on self-esteem has also made me too critical of myself and even disconnected from others because I became so immersed in my problems.

Eventually, I've discovered that self-compassion, rather than self-esteem, is what helped me get through times in my life when I thought I had hit rock bottom. When I was jobless and going through a break-up, I felt all kinds of negative emotions: anger, frustration, disappointment, and helplessness. I was able to let go of these negative feelings by connecting with humanity and being kinder to myself, which is the foundation for self-compassion—the notion that all human beings deserve compassion, kindness, and understanding.

Self-compassion seeks clarity and understanding by examining the individual in the context of the rest of humanity: looking at the experiences, environment, and culture that the individual is subjected to. This makes self-compassion far less judgmental and more forgiving. Unlike self-esteem, self-compassion is unconditional: it isn't dependent on external circumstances and is always available. According to Dr. Kristin Neff, author of *Self-Compassion*, studies have shown that in comparison to self-esteem, "self-compassion is associated with greater emotional resilience, more accurate self-concepts, more caring relationship behavior, as well as less narcissism and reactive anger."

There are many ways to learn how to become more self-compassionate. Here are some ways that I've found helpful:

Embrace your negative emotions

Don't be so hard on yourself. Let yourself know that it's okay to have negative emotions—it's all part of the human experience. It helps us learn and grow. The goal is not to dispel these feelings entirely, but to learn how to moderate and understand them. In doing so, we may become more adept at navigating through our emotional whirlwind. Accepting that it's part of the human experience to have fears, doubts, and setbacks has helped me to be more forgiving with myself. A very helpful book that walked me through the negative feelings that I was having is a guided meditation book called *Lovingkindness: The Revolutionary Art of Happiness* by Sharon Salzberg.

Understand how counterintuitive it is to be hard on yourself

Whenever you berate yourself for not meeting certain expectations, you'll end up feeling less confident and drained. Being hard on yourself is a form of self-bullying. It's essentially beating you up for no good reason. Focusing on self-esteem sets people up for this kind of mentality.

Connect with humanity

Although we all live separate lives, we share common human experiences such as pain, love, loss and triumph. These experiences take place at different points in our lives, as life is a long journey. When you can see that we belong to the same humanity, you will have more compassion and acceptance towards yourself and others. It helps reading stories about others and relating to their experiences, such as reading Humans of New York posts.

Appreciate your circumstance

Sometimes, I get so engrossed in my problems that I forget that I'm not alone in my experience and that the rest of the world is also suffering. When hearing stories about people who are in extreme and dire circumstances, you become more grateful for your blessings. Try reading stories about people whose freedoms are restricted or when their survival is at stake. Not only do these add perspective to your life, but you also gain further appreciation for the strength of the human spirit. Know that so much power lies within you. Some memoirs and biographies about survival: *Half the Sky, The Glass Castle, Escape* and *Twelve Years a Slave*. (I'm sure there's plenty more.)

Find meaning in life through living your values

Certain things in life cannot satisfy your ego, including wealth, fame, people's validation, and of course, self-esteem. These things are grounds for me, to compare myself with others.

In doing so, it makes me feel more miserable. Instead, empower yourself by taking control over your self-worth and happiness, by living according to your values, as these things do not depend on external factors.

Accept the world as it is

Our ideals and expectations can also be a source of unhappiness because reality doesn't quite match up. Sometimes we need to use our Extroverted Intuition to help us embrace the universe for what it is with all of its imperfections. Just acknowledging the imperfections of the world, accepting that reality does not always align with our ideals, and appreciating what's good in life (in spite of everything else, can help dissolve certain negative feelings).

Practice mindfulness

As introverts and idealists, we may get so lost in our thoughts that we forget to come back to earth. Sometimes we need to be reminded to enjoy the simple pleasures in life, such as savoring a good meal, going for a walk in nature, or simply paying attention to what's happening in our immediate environment. *The Book of Awesome*, by Neil Pasricha, has many great examples of the little joys in life that are often overlooked. Getting out of our heads can help put an end to the stress that comes with negative overthinking—and makes sure we don't walk into a puddle or bump into people because we're so busy contemplating.

Acknowledge your contributions

INFPs need to feel our lives are more than just ourselves. We don't want to end up feeling like our lives made no difference to anyone. So whenever I leave an impact on someone's life (whether it'd be a person, an animal, or even a tree), I feel like I'm making a difference in the world. Sometimes that's all it takes for you to see your value and purpose.

I believe that one of the perks of being an INFP is that we are highly emotionally intelligent and empathetic. Thanks to our Fi-Ne dynamic, we can put ourselves in other people's shoes and experience the world from their perspective, which in turn gives us a deeper insight into ourselves and our relations with the world. This allows us to see that we are a part of a bigger picture in this universe. By connecting with humanity in this way, we become more forgiving and self-compassionate. So, focus on self-compassion rather than self-esteem. Doing so will help you let go of the negative emotions that are holding you back from living your life and experiencing meaning and joy.

Chapter 8.

The empath's burden

"But sometimes your light attracts moths and your warmth attracts parasites."
— Warsan Shire

INFPs are considered empaths: We are highly sensitive individuals who have an innate ability to feel and perceive other people's energies and emotions intuitively. This allows us to peel away the public façade that people display and reveal their innermost feelings. This ability comes from our Fi, which enables us to look inwards, giving us a core understanding of ourselves and a heightened awareness of our emotions. We also use our Fi (combined with our Ne) to look inwards when it comes to our relationships with others. It brings us great joy to help others to unravel their inner core and learn more about who they truly are. Because of this, we tend to be great listeners and natural therapists.

As idealists, we also believe that the world should be a kinder and more compassionate place. Many of us have experienced hurt and injustices in our lives, which may trigger in us to go into the hero mode. When this happens, we want to save others, to further our belief in promoting the greater good. Because we can relate to other people's suffering, we are easily compelled to tend to their wounds.

The downside of being an empath

Although being empathetic is one of our strengths, through which we bring healing and inspiration to the world, it can also be our downside. We often encounter troubles that are associated with being an empath. Because we listen and genuinely care, we get taken advantage of. Here's a list of challenges, based on my experiences as an INFP empath, that other empaths may also likely encounter.

Being able to see the solution to people's problems which they can't see

INFP empaths are doctors in a sense: We have deep insights about other people and what their ailments are; we know what's bothering people at their core and we may also have the prescription to cure them. Others may be unable to see themselves through the same lens and so are un-open to accepting our help and wisdom, which may leave us feeling ignored and isolated.

Entering an unhealthy relationship in the hope of saving the other person

We may find ourselves gravitating towards people

who we see as damaged and in need of repair. We may commit to a relationship to save our partner even though we know that it's not the ideal relationship—but we think the good that may come out of it is worth all the trouble.

Being an emotional dumping ground for others

People are comfortable sharing their intimate problems with us because we have an aura of understanding and trust. We become someone's emotional dumping ground—they do all the talking while we do all the listening. However, we can only do this in moderation as we may find ourselves worn out from carrying too much of other people's emotional baggage. This makes us feel under-appreciated for the healing that we can bring.

Experiencing hurt in an unmutual relationship

We can find ourselves in one-sided relationships and become very absorbed by another person's world. We can care a great deal about them only to discover that the reverse doesn't always happen, which makes us melancholy and lonely.

Spreading yourself too thin when trying to save the world

As idealists who want to make the world a better place, we may find ourselves burning out from all of our endeavors when it comes to trying to save others.

Second guessing yourself and being quick to accept blame

We may also be very hard on ourselves because we feel accountable and responsible for many things that are beyond our control, including other people's happiness.

Finding it difficult to leave a bad relationship because of your ideals

We also have a tendency to idealize and romanticize our relationships, in which we only see the best qualities in others. The downside to this is that we struggle to reconcile our ideals with the reality of our lives, so we become extremely dissatisfied once our bubble has popped and reality sets in. Our deeply-felt, sincere love for our relationships and dislike of conflict also keeps us loyal, even though we feel dissatisfied.

Not saving yourself first

We may hesitate to save ourselves first because we think that doing so is selfish, which is not the case. Know how important it is to take care of yourself first, to be able to help others. Sometimes, there is only so much you can do for others; you might even be doing everyone a disservice by stepping over boundaries. To truly help others, show them how they can help themselves by setting a good example. I've also come to learn that the problem with putting others first is that you've taught them that you come second.

So save yourself the trouble and learn where to draw the line. Realize that you can't save people and can only love them. If you want to make a positive difference in the world, take care of yourself first as you can't pour anything from an empty cup.

The dangers of attracting narcissists

Before I end this chapter, I would like to warn all INFP empaths out there about our propensity to attract toxic and dangerous people such as narcissists. Why do we allow such harmful people into our lives? It's often because we like to be crusaders and try to save others from their miseries by tending to their wounds. A core trait about narcissists is that they have been hurt at some point in their life; and due to this, they will constantly and very desperately seek validation. As healers, we may have very easily bonded with narcissists in an attempt to eradicate their pain, especially if we are not consciously aware of the need to set boundaries.

Narcissists are predators: They are takers and will draw the life and soul out of the people whom they target. They want to be in control by manipulating others, and to put them down to feed their insatiable ego. The relationship between an empath and a narcissist is extremely toxic. Empaths are healers, and the more love and care we offer, the stronger the narcissist will become. Once we are no longer a source of supply for them, they will discard us and depreciate our sense of self in the process.

We shouldn't feel foolish or worthless for falling prey to narcissists. They are professional con artists. It's their trade to be able to deceive others into thinking they are someone who they aren't. They are extremely good at charming people and putting them on a pedestal as a way to lure their target. Once their victims are hooked, they will play games with them through lies and manipulation to confuse them, make them feel desperate and even worthless. Narcissists want you to loathe yourself, to make them feel better; they want to see you hurt and want to control your emotions. The best way to deal with a narcissist is to break free from all contact and walk away. Know that you are stronger and wiser than ever because of this experience.

As for myself, I am thankful that I've gotten out of the situation where a narcissist emotionally manipulated me. Why didn't I see the warning signs sooner? Well, even though I suspected something was wrong, I gave my narcissist the benefit of the doubt. I stopped listening to my Introverted Feeling; instead, I allowed my imagination to get too carried away— trying to see the potential good in everyone.

I believe our Fi can help prevent us from being exploited by toxic individuals because it tells us when someone is not being genuine and is a potential threat. *Don't turn off these warning signs. Listen to your heart.* If something feels off, it is. Our feelings can tell us a lot of truth which logic fails to do. For us, logic is only a tool that could help explain and validate what we already know deep down. It shouldn't be used to persuade our feelings (especially when something feels wrong); rather, it should only be used to serve its purpose further. So don't doubt your feelings. They are there for a reason. While you're exploring and expanding your world view with your Ne, entertaining different possibilities, also be mindful of what feels right deep inside.

My experience has also made me realize that although I'd like to believe that there is good in everyone, some people are simply cruel. INFPs value honesty and like to assume that most people are honest. Unfortunately, this makes us quite gullible; not everyone thinks the way we do and everyone has a different agenda. This is the reality of the world that we live in. I do not regret my experience even though it has been awful. This was something that I had to learn the hard way. Hopefully, I can prevent this from happening to other INFP empaths by spreading awareness. I seriously think that there should be a warning sign in our personality description so that this doesn't happen as often. (I'm aware how common this is, based on what I've observed in the INFP Facebook groups and other online forums.)

I firmly believe that we shouldn't hold grudges against these kinds of people. It will only take a toll on our emotional energy—and that's precisely what they want us to experience. I do not want to give them the pleasure of ruining me; this in itself is motivation for me to move on. Instead of taking our encounters with them too personally, I'd like to think of it as an accident. For whatever reason, such as genetics or environmental, some people have developed a cruel disposition, and we were unfortunate to have been one of their targets. (I realize that there are varying degrees of narcissism and sociopathy, but I've decided to lump them together for the purpose of conveying the core message in this chapter.)

Trying to expose them may put us in greater danger because they can be extremely vengeful and manipulative; the best we can do is to change ourselves to prevent this from happening again. If you've ever felt frustrated by an abuser who always seems to escape justice and karma, I find the excerpt below, written by an anonymous writer from *psychopathfree.com*, to be very comforting and reassuring:

"Imagine waking up every morning with an overwhelming boredom that plagues your every waking thought. Imagine never being able to enjoy any form of consistency or happiness because of that nagging boredom. Imagine looking at your 'friends' and 'loved ones' and seeing nothing more than objects to use at your disposal—jesters for your daily entertainment. Imagine feeling no connection whatsoever to those people, beyond what they can offer you at this particular moment. Imagine being unable to feel love, vulnerability, trust, and compassion. Imagine the only highs in your life come from sex, drugs, and conning people. Imagine every one of your relationships following an identical pattern, leaving behind a trail of destruction and confusion that you carefully planned. Never, not for one second, feeling or experiencing the beautiful things all around us that make this life worth living."

The perks of being an INFP empath is that we are the opposite of narcissists and sociopaths. INFPs, in general, are very spiritual and have profound compassion and an appreciation for nature, beauty, and all of those things that make life worth living. Some people, especially sociopaths, do not have that and are hollow inside. It's hard to see when they're waving their "happy" life around for everyone to see, but the very core of a sociopath's existence is justice enough. So, we should be grateful that we can live a life full of love and compassion.

Chapter 9.

INFPs and romantic relationships

"The course of true love never did run smooth."
– **William Shakespeare**

My two cents on relationships

You might wonder why I've placed this section under "The troubles in an INFP's life." Are romantic relationships part of our troubles? Not necessarily. But there are challenges for INFPs and people in general in this department.

My thoughts on relationships, in general, are that people often feel that an intimate relationship can help solve their problems and fill a void. And since they have not found that special someone, a part of them is missing. However, I believe that relationships can't fill the void and it's unhealthy to think that they will.

Longing for a relationship is a source of misery and only makes matters worse. It only focuses our attention on the part of us that feels empty, rather than helping us see ourselves as a complete and whole human being. It also sets us up for disappointment if we don't live up to our relationship expectations. In my honest opinion, swiping through Tinder all day is not worth your time.

I know people that have found a happy relationship through these dating apps and sites. But for the most part, I find that you're more likely to have success by allowing these things to happen naturally as you live your life and focus on yourself. Take a class, get a friend's referral, or participate in an event. The chances of interacting with another human being is much higher, and you're doing something that benefits your personal development and builds your confidence. You won't find yourself bored or disappointed for not finding that special someone as other things occupy you. In the past, I found myself developing relationships when I least expect; I've had much more success when I put myself out there and trying different activities than I did when I wasted hours on dating apps.

I am currently single as I'm writing this book. I'm feeling a bit alone, but I do not envy those who are in a relationship as I've also been on the other side of the fence. There are benefits to being in relationships as much as there are challenges. Relationships are only part of the journey in our personal growth, but it's not the end goal. It's there to help us learn more about ourselves and not to fill the emptiness that we may experience (as we can still feel alone in our relationships). I'd rather be alone, than to find myself in an unhealthy or stale relationship.

However, I do believe that, as social creatures, human connection is vital to our well-being and that healthy relationships should be cherished. I am a fan of Aristotle's *Nichomachean Ethics*, where Aristotle describes that a person's relationship with their partner or friend is a perception of their being. In other words, we learn about ourselves through observing the actions of those within our intimate social circle. This also ties with the Japanese proverb, "When a character of a man is not clear to you, look at his friends." If we make good choices when it comes to our friendships and intimate relationships, we can become healthier human beings because our relationships enable us to cultivate our virtues, such as generosity, kindness and patience.

My two-year relationship with my ex was happy for the most part, as we shared similar values and we worked together to become better people. Although, it did not last due to personal circumstances because I often overlook problems in my relationships and find myself dissatisfied when the truth hits. Regardless, we both learned a lot about ourselves from the relationship and I cherish the good memories that we shared. When it comes to friendships and relationships, not all of them last; and for the longest part of my life, it is hard to accept this fact. However, I've learned that life just keeps going and as mentioned, brooding over the past won't get us anywhere. As Stephen Chboksy, author of *The Perks of Being a Wallflower* says, "Things change. And friends leave. Life doesn't stop for anybody."

After breaking off my long-term relationship, I realized how much sacrifice I've made. I gave my whole heart to someone, devoting myself entirely to the relationship, instead of focusing on myself and my personal development. I am aware that this is a common problem for INFPs. We often wear our heart on our sleeves and become very altruistic, caring for another person deeply at the expense of our well-being. So, despite my painful heartbreak, breaking off my relationship gave me a breath of fresh air. I could restart my life since I had more time to myself. I had more time and energy to meet different people, try new activities, and to focus on my ambitions and career. Being on my own also gave me more clarity and time to reflect on my personal values and goals.

As far as other INFPs' relationships go, I won't be examining our dynamics with other types beyond what I've lightly touched on in the first section. I don't believe that there is one type that is perfect for us, though we might find that certain types complement each other, better than others.

For instance, we may find ourselves connecting better with other Intuitives, who can understand our abstract way of seeing the world, or those who can bond over our shared values. We might also be drawn to personalities that have a strong Extroverted Thinking function because they bring a sense of stability and security in our lives. One thing to note is that INFPs may have difficulty finding common grounds with personalities that have a strong Ti, such as INTPs and ISTPs, since their values quite differ from Fi users. Either way, learning about other types can help us connect with them better as we familiarize ourselves with their different perspectives and communication needs. However, other factors such as trust, communication, and maturity also determine the health of a relationship between any two types.

Stumbling blocks in a relationship

Many of the relationship struggles that INFPs often encounter have been mentioned throughout this book—particularly when I discuss our challenges with communication and the burden that comes with being an empath. To summarize, below is a list of common romantic relationship problems for INFPs:

- Waiting indefinitely to take the initiative with our love interests and, instead, imagine the relationship taking place in our fantasies

- Idealizing our relationships to the point where we confuse a real person with the image of them we've created in our minds

- Losing ourselves in our relationships by devoting ourselves entirely to the notion of it

- Allowing ourselves to be treated disrespectfully in a toxic relationship

- Struggling to leave a bad relationship because we're afraid of conflict and change

As you might notice, the common relationship problems for INFPs stem from our highly idealistic view of the world combined with our intense dislike of conflict. We have a tendency to romanticize our relationships whereby we see it for what it could be, instead of for what it actually is. For instance, as we begin our relationships with someone, we may already have grandiose fantasies about what our future dream house would be like, how many children we'll have, and all the places we'll explore. If we were in a toxic relationship, we might make excuses for our partner's poor behavior instead of confronting the issue, by putting ourselves in their shoes to find reasons to justify their behavior.

So how do we get out of these situations? Although we often find ourselves living in a dream world in which we see things for its potential, our introspection can also help us make wise decisions. By being self-aware of our tendencies to idealize people, we can better reflect on our situation whenever we feel let down by our partner.

For instance, instead of feeling revolted by the realization that our partner turns out not to be the person we've imagined, we would acknowledge that our disappointment is a consequence of our high and unrealistic standards that we've projected on them. And when we find excuses not to leave a toxic relationship, our introspection can tell us that we deserve so much better and that the situation that we're in should not be the norm.

Introspection involves giving ourselves space to reflect on our feelings and values, within the context of our reality. When something feels off, most of the time it is. So if you find yourself discomforted in your relationship, it's important to give yourself some time to reflect and make sense of your emotions before you openly discuss the issue with your partner.

It's also important to note that our proclivity to avoid conflict and to remain silent in our inner world could cause tension within our relationships. This can be easily avoided. It's essential to communicate our feelings with our partners and vice versa, in order for there to be mutual support and respect. If the problem between you and your partner continues to persist after it's been communicated and you still feel miserable, then you're likely in an unhealthy relationship.

One way to help you make a tough decision in a relationship, is the 10/10/10 framework invented by business writer Suzy Welch. It involves thinking about our decisions on three different time frames:

- How will we feel about it 10 minutes from now?

- How about 10 months from now?

- How about 10 years from now?

The three time frames provide an elegant way of forcing us to get some distance on our decisions.

If you find there are flaws in your relationship that you can live with, or that you and your partner are working together to fix them, then maybe the challenge is to learn to be more accepting of your relationship and its imperfections. However, if you can't see yourself being happy in the future with this relationship, then it's probably not the right one.

When it comes to finding a partner, many INFPs would look for the Prince Charming or Cinderella type, but it's not the real thing. What we should really look for in a partner is someone who is passionate about what they do, who strives to become a better person, who challenges us intellectually, who respects and appreciates us, who makes us feel supported, and who can help show us that real life is not a fairytale but can still be amazing.

Chapter 10.

The lonely INFP

"There are places and moments in which one is so completely alone that one sees the world entire."
– *Jules Renard*

It's not uncommon for INFPs to experience loneliness and periods of depression. We often feel alone and isolated because of the way we see the world. Our dominant Fi makes us keep our deeply held values and feelings private and invisible from the outside world. This is because Fi is individuating, and our subjective experiences are disconnected from the rest of the world. We are often isolated in our thoughts and inner world, and struggle to articulate them and make them known. Sometimes, my loneliness and depression also stem from being utterly lost; I experienced an existential crisis and was losing touch with who I was in relation to the world. Other times, I feel isolated when I'm surrounded by people who misunderstand me and are oblivious to my inner-most thoughts and feelings. This chapter will explore and embrace these feelings and hope to give them some new light.

Coping with loneliness

Although loneliness holds a negative connotation and is often associated with depression, it's not entirely bad. Loneliness is a human condition. Sometimes I find solace from being alone in my thoughts. I'm not advocating that we should feel lonely, as it's not a pleasant state to be in, but I believe it can also be good for us at times. And truthfully, I often can't help but feel lonely and so I am learning to embrace this condition. Below are some quotes that I've found helpful when it comes to embracing loneliness.

"Loneliness is the human condition. Cultivate it. The way it tunnels into you allows your soul room to grow. Never expect to outgrow loneliness. Never hope to find people who will understand you, someone to fill that space. An intelligent, sensitive person is the exception, the very great exception. If you expect to find people who will understand you, you will grow murderous with disappointment. The best you'll ever do is to understand yourself, know what it is that you want, and not let the cattle stand in your way."

*— **Janet Fitch***

"Deep in my heart I know that I am a loner. I have tried to blend in with the world and be sociable, but the more people I meet, the more disappointed I am. So, I've learned to enjoy myself."
— **Steven Aitchison**

"Alone always felt like an actual place to me, as if it weren't a state of being, but rather a room where I could retreat to be who I really was."
– **Cheryl Strayed**

"Loneliness adds beauty to life. It puts a special burn on sunsets and makes night air smell better."
— **Henry Rollins**

"Perhaps only people who are capable of real togetherness have that look of being alone in the universe. The others have a certain stickiness; they stick to the mass."
— **D.H. Lawrence**

"Remember: the time you feel lonely is the time you most need to be by yourself. Life's cruelest irony."
— Douglas Coupland

"Music was my refuge. I could crawl into the space between the notes and curl my back to loneliness."
— Maya Angelou

"When I get lonely these days, I think: So BE lonely, Liz. Learn your way around loneliness. Make a map of it. Sit with it, for once in your life. Welcome to the human experience. But never again use another person's body or emotions as a scratching post for your own unfulfilled yearnings."
— Elizabeth Gilbert

"We must become so alone, so utterly alone, that we withdraw into our innermost self. It is a way of bitter suffering. But then our solitude is overcome, we are no longer alone, for we find that our innermost self is the spirit, that it is

God, the indivisible. And suddenly we find ourselves in the midst of the world, yet undisturbed by its multiplicity, for our innermost soul we know ourselves to be one with all being."
— Hermann Hesse

*"When you're surrounded by all these people, it can be lonelier than when you're by yourself. You can be in a huge crowd, but if you don't feel like you can trust anyone or talk to anybody, you feel like you're really alone." — **Fiona Apple***

"There is a pleasure in the pathless woods; There is a rapture on the lonely shore; There is a society where none intrudes, By the deep Sea, and music in its roar: I love not Man the less, but Nature more."
— Lord Byron

*"Some nights are made for torture, or reflection, or the savoring of loneliness." — **Poppy Z. Brite***

"If you are alone you belong entirely to yourself. If you are accompanied by even one companion, you belong only half to yourself or even less in proportion to the thoughtlessness of his conduct and if you have more than one companion you will fall more deeply into the same plight."

— **Leonardo da Vinci**

"The moment when we are most alone is when we embrace another's loneliness." — **Mitch Albom**

"Use loneliness. Its ache creates urgency to reconnect with the world. Take that aching and use it to propel you deeper into your need for expression, your need to speak, to say who you are."

— **Natalie Goldberg**

"There are some places in life where you can only go alone. Embrace the beauty of your solo journey."

— **Mandy Hale**

I can even recall some blissful moments when I'm alone in my thoughts. There's a kind of peacefulness and clarity that comes with it. I enjoy moments when I'm looking out of the window from a long road trip, marveling at the scenery and reflecting on my thoughts. Sometimes, I enter a nearly transcendental state, in which I feel deeply connected to something that is divine—these moments can only take place when I'm in my inner world. So I truly believe there is a beauty to loneliness and it is something that can be embraced.

Experiencing depression

Although I've suggested that loneliness is something that we can embrace, if we go for long periods of time feeling alone, we might end up depressed. As an INFP, I find that I do enter a depression every few years or so. I've come to accept this as a normal part of my life (in a good way). Also, please be advised that I am not an expert on this subject matter and I'm only speaking from my personal experiences; so if you find that your condition is chronic, please seek professional help.

I'm aware that many INFPs also struggle with depression. We may find ourselves in a rut in which we cannot make that connection between our external realities and our inner world. As a consequence, we are unable to establish meaning in our lives. We may even reach a point where we lose touch with ourselves. For instance, one time I was so immersed in my philosophy studies that I ended up feeling lost and detached. I became so removed from my reality that I felt as if I was lost in a mumble jumble of abstract thoughts that only further distanced me from the truth that I was seeking.

The story behind my bouts of depression is that it usually takes place at a point in my life where I have burned out from doing whatever I was doing. My goals no longer made sense and I find myself feeling completely lost. I exhausted all of my functions and they are no longer helpful. I lost touch with my Introverted Feeling, and no longer feel certain about my purpose in life. My Extroverted Intuition fails to give me useful input from the external word, and my Introverted Sensing tries to find something that has worked before in the past but it's no longer useful. I then end up exhausting my Extroverted Thinking, which only makes matters worse, because I end up forcing myself to do something that I'm not passionate about. For instance, I would convince myself that I will be better off if I focused on school, blocking off my entire week to do drudgery tasks, instead of allowing myself to try something more rejuvenating.

But things do get better. My trick is to allow myself to shut down, give myself a rest, and not to get so boggled up and frustrated for feeling this way. This means taking things slow and easy; and eventually, I'll come across something, an idea or activity, that I am passionate about. I can't force these things to happen since it will only make me more exasperated. To regain balance, it helps to try to get in touch with my Introverted Feeling by finding activities that facilitates expression of feelings, such as music, dance, and writing.

If you find yourself feeling burned out and possibly depressed, here are some thoughts:

Tell yourself it's okay. Relax. Don't worry. It's going to be fine. Your system is just rebooting itself, like a computer. You might be going through an existentialist crisis: feeling lost, losing touch with reality, losing touch with yourself and with your internal values. It happens. I find that depressions are like illnesses that can go away with time. It doesn't go away when you want it to. It'll naturally run its course, and then you'll find something new and enlightening as you leave this life phase.

Just let it flow. Turn off your screen. Go for nature walks. Listen to music. Find something random to do. Pick up a book. Travel.

Eventually, you'll find that meaning that you've been longing for. You don't know what it is yet, but it's there. Because deep down, you can feel that you have a lot of energy that wants to be unleashed; it just hasn't found the right time and place, but it'll happen.

In the meantime, an easy way to ground yourself is to open up your senses, be present in the physical world, get in touch with your body, and don't think too hard. Go for a run. Try a dance or fitness class. I find that engaging in such activities is helpful when it comes to recover from depression.

The light is on the other side, and your life is going to be very exciting. So like I said, just take it easy for now.

Part III

The career path of an INFP

"It is a rough road that leads to the heights of greatness."
– Lucius Annaeus Seneca

Chapter 11.

INFP vs. Reality

"To be yourself in a world that is constantly trying to make you something else is the greatest accomplishment."
– Ralph Waldo Emerson

For a dreamer, the real world can be a dull and unpleasant place, compared to the beauty and visions found within our imagination. For instance, I dislike talking about the nitty-gritty details of daily life. Conversations about finance, chores, and even the news, can be irksome and tiring and are droning sounds to my psyche. At times, I find myself escaping from such conversations and drifting into a different universe, contemplating and exploring the various thoughts and emotions that run through my stream of consciousness. While I'm in this dream world, everything seems much more ideal and pleasant.

However, I find that my imagination can get too carried away at times, where I struggle to find that right balance between my idealism and reality. There were so many things that I wanted to do: such as starting a philosophy school for children, becoming a lounge pianist at a 5-star hotel, and owning two dogs (at the time when I was young). I was restricted from achieving my many visions because I was inhibited by my reality. Not only did I have too many ideas, but it was also hard for me to actualize my dreams because I wasn't always good at being practical.

So, every day it would seem like it's me vs. the rest of the world. Me vs. reality. It's an uphill battle to find that right balance between living my dreams and making things happen. Sometimes I even find myself surrendering to the demands of reality, settling for a job or a career path that holds little meaning to me, but seems to be the most practical option. I often find that I can only go so long doing something that I'm not passionate about before I run dry and find myself in a ditch. For this reason, it is important that I have that space, that breather where my creativity and imagination can run wild and be expressed freely to preserve my mental well-being. To this day, I am forever grateful to have my piano as an outlet and a place for me to express my innermost feelings and thoughts, during those times when I feel as if I am suffocated by the rest of the world.

You might wonder, can INFPs find fulfillment in the real world? INFPs have an inner flame and a burning desire to reach our potential, to create an impression in this world. For many of us, we don't only want this to happen in our dreams. The reason why I devoted this entire section on the career path of an INFP is that I've noticed a common challenge with INFPs when it comes to finding meaning in the work that we do. Is it possible to find a satisfying career path while still being an idealist? Absolutely.

In the next few chapters, I'll share my career journey, and how I found the place where my skills and interests align. But most importantly, I'll share the lessons that I've learned and the thought processes that I've gone through, to help get me to where I am today.

Chapter 12.

An unexpected journey

*"When one door closes, another
one opens."*
– Alexander Graham Bell

Throughout my life, I've had many interests, which
made it difficult to pick a career path. For instance, in
high school, I wanted to become a biomedical
engineer. In fact, in Grade 11, I was even selected to
be a participant in Shad Valley, a competitive science
and entrepreneur summer program offered for
exceptional high school students. However, after
finishing my diploma, I lost interest in this field as I
no longer found a career path in biomedical
engineering fulfilling.

When I enrolled in university, I had no idea what to
major in, so I took a variety of courses until I
stumbled across something that inspired me.
Eventually, I found myself studying philosophy.
Learning about this subject opened my world. I loved
contemplating the meaning of life and understanding

the depths of humanity. From reading Aristotle to Nietzsche to de Beauvoir, I felt like I was exploring a treasure chest of knowledge. Although studying philosophy changed my life, in my final years of study, my romance with this subject was coming to an end. I was tired out from all of the abstract thinking and I wanted to ground myself again. In doing so, I ended up trying to pursue more practical career paths.

Majoring in philosophy also made me anxious about my career prospects. My Te responded by compelling me to pick more "practical" courses to minor in, such as political science and probability and statistics... only to discover that I didn't enjoy them. I've even considered going to law school or becoming a policy analyst, based on the route that other philosophy majors have taken after they graduated. So I applied to a few public policy graduate programs, only to have my application denied by each one. I was devastated at the time.

Retrospectively, I'm so glad that I was rejected from these programs: I'm so much happier with my current career choice in marketing. I would have been in a rut had I settled for a career that did not allow me to be creative and flexible.

Opening up to new opportunities

Even though I had many dreams and visions for myself at different points in life, I don't consider myself a failure nor do I regret any of my choices. I'm proud of what I've been able to accomplish. And I owe all of my successes to being flexible and pursuing short-term goals that spark my interest at the time. All of my varying pursuits led me down to another exciting path of self-discovery and growth.

For instance, if it weren't for my early interest in the sciences, I wouldn't have met some amazing connections and friends from my Shad Valley science program. If I didn't study philosophy, I wouldn't have the same confidence in my analytical skills and writing abilities. All of my experiences were invaluable and gave me the tools and insight to get to the next step.

For INFPs, the problem with our imagination is that it can be hard to align it with our reality. We might envision doing things that are not tangible, but that doesn't mean that they don't serve any purpose. My imagination inspires me to take on new ventures, even though what I end up doing may be completely different than what I had initially intended. It used to frustrate me that I could not realize my long-term plans, including picking the perfect career. I now know that I thrive when I look for opportunities in the present, rather than creating more set plans for myself. I make the most of my time when I am living in the moment and picking up new information and inspiration as I go.

In fact, being flexible and adaptable is one of our greatest strengths. As Charles Darwin says, "It is not the strongest of the species that survives, nor the most intelligent; it is the one most adaptable to change." Thus it's extremely important for us to continue to engage with the external world and make new discoveries, using our perceiving function, instead of staying too long in our inner world.

Our Ne enables us to look at possibilities and to form ideas by taking in information from the external world. We work best when we find new ways to enact our inner values. For instance, Newton Scamander, a fictional INFP character from J.K. Rowling's *Fantastic Beasts and Where to Find Them*, uses his Extroverted Intuition to make new discoveries and find solutions to help magical creatures.

A good way to think about using your Ne is to consider yourself an explorer. You don't necessarily need to know what you'll do for the rest of your life, but that doesn't mean you can't find success. Take Kirstine Stewart, author of *Our Turn* and former VP Media at Twitter, for example. She attributes her career success to her "openness to new opportunities, however, unpredictable or unexpected." She said she learned to love the job she stumbled into. The more possibilities you open yourself to, the greater the chance you'll find something that will put your talents to work. Although it may seem scary to live life with uncertainty, this gives our life variety. If we knew everything that was going to happen in our lives, then our lives would be boring. It's also a very important skill to be adaptable to the changes of the world. Plans often go awry because life is full of surprises.

Learning about new things also brings great joy and meaning to me. Even though I've started out this section complaining about my struggles with reality, the truth is that reality is also the place where I can live authentically and find real happiness—it's something that has to be lived, not simply imagined. As Jon Krakauer, author of *Into the Wild*, says, "It is the experiences, the memories, the great triumphant joy of living to the fullest extent, in which real meaning is found."

Some of my best memories at university, for instance, were from the clubs that I've joined. I was an executive for the McGill Students for UN Women National Committee and had such a worthwhile experience meeting like-minded individuals, organizing film screenings, participating in coffee meet-ups, and volunteering for events. I felt like I was using my creativity, values, and introspection to create an impact in society.

It's okay to take the unconventional road

It's important not to allow ourselves to succumb to the pressures of society. We live in a world where people associate success by the size of our paychecks, the title of our jobs, and the wealth of our connections, among other external things. As INFPs we often feel pressured to provide an absolute answer to "What do you want to do with your life?" These kinds of thoughts and questions only build our anxiety and are counterproductive for us. We might react negatively, as I have in many instances, by allowing our inferior Extroverted Thinking to take control of the steering wheel. This prevents us from pursuing our passions. We end up choosing a more "pragmatic" route that, which sets us up for depression.

It's fallacious to assume that we need to have an answer to this question to find success in life. As you have probably seen, many accomplished people in our society have found their careers through experimenting and adapting to change. I like the statement made by Jaime Casap, Google Global Education Evangelist:

> *"Don't ask kids what they want to be when they grow up, but what problems do they want to solve. This changes the conversation from who do I want to work for, to what do I need to learn to be able to do that."*

Framing the question this way is far more constructive since it focuses on the solution rather than the result. This also takes away the labels and titles that people aspire to have, without giving a thought as to whether they'd enjoy the process that it entails. Take me, for instance. Being a lawyer or a biomedical engineer were my aspirational careers at some point, but I found out that I didn't enjoy the actual work that's involved to get there.

Nevertheless, even though our plans change over the course of time, it's still essential to have goals in life in order to progress. Without a goal, project or an aim, you can find yourself in limbo—I can speak from my experience that it's not a very pleasant state to be in. Your goal is something that gives your life meaning, in which you're directing your ambitions and values—your Introverted Feeling—towards what the world has to offer. Hence, it's essential to keep striving while adapting to change.

And if you feel like you've hit rock bottom because you don't have a sense of direction, I highly recommend listening to J.K. Rowling's Harvard commencement speech. This speech had motivated me when I was going through my career limbo. Here's an inspiring quote from the speech:

> *"Your qualifications, your CV, are not your life. Life is difficult, and complicated, and beyond anyone's total control, and the humility to know that will enable you to survive its vicissitudes."*

Life is indeed challenging, where we each have our struggles. So don't be hard on yourself if you find yourself in a rut, as we've either all been there or will be. You might feel deterred by those who seem to have found their way and have accomplished more. I remember feeling inadequate when I saw my peers succeeding in their competitive and specialized programs, such as business and engineering, while I was lost and floundering with an undecided major. However, I believe we're each creating our own unique pathway. I've discovered that I don't live fully when I follow someone else's pathway. On the other hand, when I focus on what I want in life, I get more out of it.

Chapter 13.

Lessons from the real world

"Don't be afraid to take an unfamiliar path. Sometimes they're the ones that take you to the best places" – **Unknown**

Although I have now found a career, things weren't easy after I graduated and it was a real uphill battle. I think one of the hardest challenges for INFPs is finding a career path that not only interests us, but also pays the bills. To be honest with you, it wasn't until my fifth business card and a variety of side jobs that I've finally landed my current career.

Knocking on doors

When it comes to finding a career, we often have to start from scratch and do the grunt work. The world doesn't owe us for our uniqueness and talents. We may be talented, but if we don't put in the effort to make use of it, we won't go far. As Stephen King says, "Talent is cheaper than table salt. What separates the talented individual from the successful one is a lot of hard work." And, sometimes, our worst jobs teach us so much and provide a groundwork for us to establish a successful career path.

My career journey in the "real world" began after I graduated from university. After being denied entry into graduate school, I was once again completely lost. I ended up applying for a variety of entry-level job postings over the summer to no avail. By fall time, I thought I found my lucky break when I received a phone call from a hiring manager for a "marketing" position. What it ended up being was a commission-only door-to-door sales job, and I was making even less than minimum wage.

The job was very demanding and didn't give me time to relax, or even have lunch since that means hitting fewer doors and potentially less sales. Some days I would be outside in the freezing rain or chase buses and run into a puddle to make it back to the office in time. And often I would upset some people for interrupting them and invading their space; occasionally, I would get yelled at and escorted outside.

The funny thing is, even though it was a terrible job, I was somehow convinced that it was a great opportunity, especially since I was told that many new recruits were successful and climbed to a management position within weeks (which isn't true, since the turnover rate is extremely high). So I ended

up knocking on doors for about a month until it
finally made sense for me to quit.

What my "worst" job taught me

Even though door-to-door sales is one of the worst
jobs I had, the experience helped me grow a thicker
skin. I used to tear up easily when I got yelled at by
people. But I was taught not to be reactive and take
these things personally since it's inevitable that these
things happen given the nature of the job.

In addition to learning not to take things too
personally, here are some other lessons that I learned:

–   All businesses depend on making sales to
    thrive.

–   Knowing how to sell is a highly useful skill,
    no matter what your career. Even if you're an
    author, you need to market your book to sell
    it. You might be the "best-writing" author, but
    that's not the same as being the "best-selling"
    author.

–   Sometimes you need to knock on a ton of
    doors before you see results.

–   To earn people's trust, you have to listen to
    their side of the problem.

–   The more people you meet, the more you
    learn.

I believe these life lessons are helpful for INFPs since we often get too caught up in our inner world, focusing on our values and feelings, without making connections to the real world. For instance, many of us may aspire to become artists. However, if there isn't a market for the work that we do or we don't know how to sell our service, it can't help us pay the bills. And sometimes, we reject our external realities because we're either afraid of the unknown or it conflicts with our inner values. When this happens, we find ourselves withdrawing and giving up on finding meaning in the real world. We mustn't let reality become our enemy. If we want our ideas to become a reality, we have to learn how to work with reality.

Chapter 14.

Building your career

"A journey of a thousand miles begins with a single step."
– Lao Tzu

If I had to give myself one piece of career advice, I'd say, let go of your fears and anxiety. Don't let the voice that tells you "I'm no good" and "I'm not made for this world" get in the way. I used to feel that because of high youth unemployment, capitalism, and the fact I've chosen to major in the liberal arts instead of something more technical, I didn't stand a chance in the job market.

As well, your personality, being a Feeler instead of a Thinker, a Perceiver instead of a Judger, an introvert instead of an extrovert, are also no excuses for not being able to make it in this world. Each of us brings a unique gift that is valuable to society. We need to be able to recognize this ourselves to find success since we can't assume that it'll happen without us putting in conscious effort. For many people, the real barrier to building a career is their reluctance to act and to correct the fact that they have no employable skills.

Also, one of the biggest things that I've learned is how important it is for me to celebrate the "small" wins in life. As INFPs, we are extremely hard on ourselves and far too modest, to the point where we often belittle or downplay our achievements because it feels pretentious to take full credit. This is to a fault, for we need to acknowledge our accomplishments and strengths to build confidence, reward our brain, and to showcase our accomplishments.

See where your skills and interests align

The best way to discover where your skills and interests align is to put yourself out there and be open to a broad range of experiences. That way you can discover your strengths, and find what motivates you.

For instance, I tried a number of different things, including applying to hundreds of job postings, volunteering, starting a blog, and attending networking events, until I was able to arrange all the pieces and find a career focus where my skills and interests align. I found that what motivates me is being able to share my ideas creatively and helping others through writing. Hence, the jobs that were appealing to me were marketing positions that involved writing content. Had I not applied to so many positions posted on the job board, I would not have made this discovery.

When it comes to finding your career interests, use your introspection to your advantage and ask yourself a lot of questions. Do you find that people come to you for therapy or advice? If so, would you prefer to interact face-to-face or online? Do you like to be creative and expressive most of the time? What were some examples of when you were creative in the past?

According to Isabel Myers in *Gifts Differing*, INFPs excel in fields that deal with possibilities for people, such as counseling, teaching, literature, art, science, research, and psychology. Even though INFPs are dominant Feelers, they also excel in the sciences; their success in this field may be attributed to the enthusiasm that is spurred from "intuition reaching a truth" as well as solving problems that would benefit people.

To narrow things down, it might be helpful to consider your core interests. Dr. A.J. Drenth from *Personality Junkie* has broken down career paths for INFPs to consider, based on core domains: Realistic, Investigative, Artistic, and Social. Those with **Realistic** interests prefer physical hands-on work, whereas the **Investigative** domain incorporates analytic, scientific, and academic interests. The **Artistic** domain captures those with unconventional and creative interests. And, the **Social** domain enjoys working with people.

Of course, you're not restricted to one category and can fall under multiple categories. For instance,

INFPs with Investigative-Social interests often study the social sciences such as psychology and sociology. INFPs with Investigative-Artistic interests may find themselves pursuing philosophy or computer science in school.

Below is a list of some possible career paths for INFPs based on these four interest domains, and some of them may overlap with each other; for instance, a music therapist would fall under Artistic-Social, but I've put it under social.

Realistic
- Landscape architecture
- Veterinarian
- Nutritionist
- Herbalist
- Geologist
- Interior designer
- Environmental scientist
- Translator

Investigative
- Computer scientist
- UX designer
- Librarian
- Psychiatrist/Psychologist
- Professor: social sciences or humanities and liberal arts
- Social media strategist
- Marketing specialist

Artistic
- Graphic designer

- – Architect
- – Game developer
- – Web designer
- – Copywriter/Content writer
- – Art director
- – Fashion designer
- – Professional photographer
- – Content director
- – Musician
- – Merchandise displayer

Social
- – Social scientist
- – Psychologist
- – Speech pathologist
- – Counselor
- – Holistic healthcare (e.g., acupuncture, yoga)
- – Therapist/Music Therapist
- – Teacher
- – Human resources/recruiter
- – Education consultant

Some of these careers, lean heavier on the thinking side, which places heavy demands on our inferior function. The ideal career for INFPs allows us to find the optimum balance between all of our functions: Fi, Ne, Si, and Te. So a career that allows INFPs to achieve this integration, such as music and writing are likely fulfilling. Many INFPs are gifted in language and would find themselves excelling in a career that involves writing.

A good work environment

Be sure to consider the kind of environment that you want to work in. You may want to avoid traditional work environments that have a hierarchical or bureaucratic structure since they don't allow you to express your very personal values and feelings. Fortunately, many organizations are adopting collaborative workspaces, and our society is becoming more digital, so there are more opportunities than ever for us to use our Fi.

INFPs need to be in a work environment that's flexible, fosters a sense of community, and gives us enough space to work independently. We need to have autonomy and space to concentrate without all the hustle and bustle, or else we will become drained. And even though we don't like our jobs, who we work with can also make a big difference. For instance, although my data entry job was the dullest job I've ever had, I enjoyed the people who I worked with, which made the experience so much more pleasant.

Based on my experiences, I realize that the company culture and values are more important than the type of industry that it's in. For instance, even though INFPs may find themselves drawn to non-profits and the education sector, sometimes these organizations do not have values that are aligned with yours. When I worked at a local music studio, I felt awful that the students were not getting the quality education that they deserved, because the turnover rate was extremely high. I had mixed feelings about working for non-profits since it's important to me that the donation money does not go wasted. You can learn about what other employees think of their company by looking on job review sites such as Glassdoor.

It's also important to see the value in the work that I do. For instance, when it comes to marketing, I feel motivated and inspired when I believe in the value and social benefit of the product or service that I am promoting. I'm also motivated by the knowledge that the work that I'm doing is helping me grow as a person.

However, if you're just starting off and need to get experience, you may not have that luxury to be "picky." But do eventually move on from where you're at if you don't like where you are. As Jim Rohn says, "If you don't like where you are, move. You're not a tree."

Setting realistic expectations

You might have come across a job description that sparks your interest. But sometimes, depending on the market, it's not the most viable option. Although, at one time, I wanted to be a lounge pianist, it wasn't going to help me make a living. Even industries that seem more practical such as mediation and print publishing may not be jobs that are in demand in the market. So it's very important to find the right balance between your interests and what's realistic by conducting some research. I found that the best place to research is by looking at job boards to see what's in demand and what the average salary is for a particular position. Reach out to professionals who are already in that field. You can find mentors on sites such as LinkedIn and tenthousandcoffees.com.

Here's a checklist to help you out:

- – Do you enjoy the work that's involved?
- – Do you have the skill sets for it? If not, can you learn it?
- – Will you be able to earn enough to feel satisfied? What's the average salary range?

No matter what job you find yourself in, there are always going to be aspects that are less enjoyable, since that's the nature of reality. As long as you can translate what you do into something that gives you meaning, then you're on the right track. And if you're feeling stuck, then maybe it's time to try something else and re-assess your situation, so that it does give you meaning. Even if you do not land the career that you're most passionate about, appreciate it for what it can provide: sometimes having a career gives you the learning experiences, provision, and stability that you need, so that you have the means to pursue your passions. But don't ever settle in life and stop pursuing your passions, as pursuing your passions fuels your energy and spirit.

Even though landing the ideal career is nearly impossible, because of the very word "ideal," I do feel that there are careers that INFPs can find enjoyable. I find content writing interesting, even though I'm not always excited by the product that I market; I derive satisfaction from applying my creativity, writing skills, and understanding of the human condition to create copies that can generate likes, shares, and more sales.

Making a deal with reality

As INFPs, every decision that we make is a reflection of who we are and what we believe in. So for us, the notion of selling ourselves to be marketable cheapens our individuality and personhood. It makes us seem like a commodity, someone who is valuable insofar as they can generate money. However, after my experience in sales and being struck by reality, I learned how important it is to be pragmatic. Instead of always thinking in terms of what serves your values and ideals, you have to consider what serves the system, such as capitalism. What does the market want? What skills are needed?

I've come to realize that to live according to our values, we have to be objective and buy into the system. In other words, we have to use Extroverted Thinking to support our Introverted Feeling's objective. Even if you find yourself pursuing the sciences or the social services, you are still required to do things that you may not necessary enjoy, such as applying cold hard logic to come up with a better solution for humanity.

And when it comes to your career, deep down, you probably don't care about a career. You care about your deep principles, such as the respect and admiration of your family and friends, and the feeling that the world rewards your talents.

For me, I'm so much better off today working with a full-salary than I was when I was jobless and without any sense of direction. Work brought me new experiences that I could never have if I stayed in my room. I now live in a city where I meet all kinds of people, I've attended various conferences, I'm helping people with their businesses, and I'm learning more about the world. I find purpose in my work from realizing that it ultimately serves my values and gives me a sense of pride. I want to continue to grow as a person, become more well-rounded, contribute to the economy, challenge myself, and be financially independent. My career enables me to achieve these purposes and makes my life more fulfilling.

Building your profile

When it comes to building your career profile, it's essential that you're able to clearly define your career. You need to have a target and specialize in something. When you're trying to be "everything," you're doing yourself a disservice. For instance, even though I've had a variety of experiences, from being a piano teacher to a marketing coordinator, I had to tailor my resume so that it focuses on my content writing experiences.

As well, most employers are looking for hard skills. Fortunately, for many jobs, you don't need to do too much extra schooling to acquire hard skills. With online resources, it is easy to start building specific skills without having to spend a ton of money. You can also look for internship opportunities to acquire specific skills and experiences. Have a look at the technical skills requirements on job postings and then look online for the resources to develop those skills. For instance, if you're interested in content writing, it's important to know search engine optimization (SEO) and even analytics.

Once you're ready, find concrete examples of how your skills can benefit employers and help generate revenue for their business. A great way to showcase your skills and experiences is to create a portfolio that highlights some of the projects where these skills apply. If you can't find any work experience, create it —make your own project. For instance, I started off finding freelance writing gigs on popular sites such as Fiverr, where I became a guest blogger on various sites for $5. I know $5 barely covers my lunch, but I didn't do it for the money: I did it to build my portfolio. Another great site is Etsy, where you can sell your personal designs, such as a website template or a piece of clothing that you made, to help you build your portfolio.

And don't forget to take pride in your strengths and accomplishments. As mentioned earlier, INFPs are too modest for our own good. Being too humble may give the appearance that we lack confidence and also entails downplaying our achievements. This works to our disadvantage as we need to be able to convince others that we're a worthy candidate. Here's a list of some INFP attributes:

- Creative
- Empathetic

- Cooperative
- Flexible and adaptable
- Independent
- Determined
- Analytical

Be sure to provide concrete examples to back up your claims. Here's an example: I'm able to put myself in other people's shoes to help create content that they can relate to. Because of this, I have written articles that have generated over 30,000 views and 100 shares, etc. By creating relevant content, I'm able to help your business nourish leads as well as build credibility.

When it comes to standing out from the crowd, I believe that INFPs have a great advantage because we are not the cookie cutters in this world. We are incredibly creative, and we personalize our experiences in a way that makes us unique. Also, we're genuinely interested in helping others, in ways which others can sense and appreciate. However, we often undervalue and undersell ourselves. When we do this, other people may perceive us as being less competent than what we are, which reduces our market value. So, instead, try your best to be positive and adopt a solution-oriented mindset, and be proud of what you can achieve.

The entrepreneurial INFP

Especially because INFPs value autonomy and don't like to work under strict rules and order, entrepreneurship or freelancing is also an option to consider. However, there are also lots of risks involved in running your own business that you should be aware of. It's important to know what you're getting yourself into before you decide to work for yourself. Here are three things to consider:

1. **You must regularly make sales and acquire new clients**
   The biggest challenge to running your own business is to be able to earn enough for your living. Whether you decide to freelance or to start a small business, you have to make sales on a regular basis to survive. You also have to manage your earnings and accounting to ensure that your business is profitable.

2. **You must understand your market**
   Sometimes it's not about what you want to market, but what people want. You have to find your niche and cater to their needs and interests. People need to be interested in your product or service for you to have any business.

3. **You have to work twice as hard**
   Just because you're not working from 9-5 doesn't mean that you have more free time. In fact, as a freelancer or a start-up, you need to have lots of discipline, focus, and dedication and work twice as long to get your business going.

Although running your own business can be very rewarding, it's not something that should be glamorized. I don't mean to deter you from choosing the entrepreneurial life; it can work if you put in the effort and tap into the right market. You can always give it a try without quitting your day job first before you go all out. I have a friend who used to work at my mom's warehouse where she learned a lot about running a small business; now she is quite successful running her own business selling cutesy Japanese-inspired toys at Comicons and on her website. Her career move involved slow transition, from deciding to work only part-time at our office, to quitting entirely so that she could be fully committed to her work.

As for me, as much as I like to have autonomy, I need to be in a working environment where there are people and some structure; otherwise, I can become quite lazy and disorganized. Sometimes finding that right balance is hard. Fortunately, my current company gives us some work from home days, which allows for more flexibility in my schedule. Of course, not every company offers this, so sometimes you have to make that tradeoff between flexibility and stability.

Stumbling blocks in the workplace

Every opportunity comes with its challenges. Here are some common challenges for INFPs in the workplace:

Completing repetitive and detail oriented tasks

This is indeed challenging for INFPs who prefer to

focus on the big picture. I find that we're only able to accomplish mundane tasks in small amounts before we become drained. Sometimes we have no choice but to suck it up and do things that we don't like. As long as we're able to find room to be creative and free, then we'll probably survive. My other advice would be to try to avoid careers that place a heavy demand on these kinds of tasks.

Finding variety

Building off from the previous point, sometimes we see ourselves stuck doing work that won't allow us to grow and be creative. When we are in our dominant-tertiary loop, we often allow ourselves to be confined to doing repetitive work instead of learning new things. To get out of this rut, we have to use our Extroverted Intuition to find ways in which we can try something different, whether it is to learn new skill sets, or take on new projects and challenges.

Consider conducting some research and see what's trending in your industry, and then come up with ideas to help you and your company improve. For instance, if you're a counselor, maybe you discovered facilitating certain workshops to be helpful for your patients. Or, if you work at a store, perhaps you can find creative ways to draw attention to your location and deliver better customer service. INFPs have a love for learning and discovery, and so finding new ways to challenge ourselves in our careers can be extremely fulfilling.

Setting expectations

I remember how overwhelmed I was when I first started my career and didn't set any expectations. I was managed by three different people at once and was constantly being interrupted and bombarded with more projects than I could handle. It was important for me to regain control over my schedule; I was able to do so by blocking off time for myself in my calendar and creating a spreadsheet on Google Drive so that everyone was aware that I was busy working on other projects.

Being recognized for our work

It's especially important for INFPs to feel recognized for the value that we bring to the industry. However, sometimes we can't depend on others to notice this. We might have to "brag" a little which entails mentioning some of our noteworthy accomplishments from time to time (this is also something to consider doing when we're looking for reasons for a raise).

Giving ourselves space to recharge

Not only do we need to take care of our well-being by allowing ourselves to physically recharge (which includes eating well, having enough sleep, etc.), we also need to replenish our soul with activities that can nourish your Introverted Feeling. For instance, if you find yourself spending too much time doing work that does not feed your soul, then it's time to recharge. This can be as simple as giving yourself more time for fun after work or changing the way you work. If possible, maybe you can try a new role or task. Ultimately, if your work does not give you reasonable flexibility, maybe it's time to look for a new job.

Negotiating a raise

Susan Scanlon, the editor of the *Type Reporter*, observed that Feelers are underpaid because they are too modest and less comfortable with the notion of asking for a raise. For instance, an INFP would say, "I keep asking myself 'Can they afford it?' and 'Am I really worth it?" In contrast, an INTP would say, "I don't consider negotiating a game, I consider it a point of clarification." Although money isn't everything, I believe it is important to be valued for your work in the form of compensation. Negotiating a raise is something that INFPs would find trouble with, but I believe it's worth the challenge.

Handling criticisms and feedback

Sheryl Sandberg, Chief Operating Officer at Facebook, says the number one thing she looks for in someone who can scale with a company is a person "who takes feedback well," since these are the "people who can learn and grow quickly." Being able to take feedback well poses a challenge for INFPs since this entails putting your feelings aside to learn from the situation and not letting your emotions get the best of you. This is why it's important for us to learn not to take things too personally.

Part IV

INFP and inspiration

"If you hear a voice within you say, 'You cannot paint,' then by all means paint, and that voice will be silenced." – **Vincent van Gogh**

Chapter 15.

INFP and motivation

> *"I'd be more frightened by not using whatever abilities I'd been given. I'd be more frightened by procrastination and laziness."*
> *– Denzel Washington*

This is one of the most important chapters in this book. As INFPs, we are extremely passionate, but we are often challenged to reach our goals because of our idealism. The problem for INFPs and other personality types who have strong Extroverted Intuition is that it's difficult for us to focus, because of our propensity to explore new ideas and possibilities. We become easily thrilled by bursts of new inspiration, only to lose interest once we either find what we're looking for or discover something else that captures our attention. The thing is, we get bored quite easily. This is problematic, as it prevents us from achieving our many goals and ideals. Furthermore, as intuitive introverts, we spend an awful lot of time contemplating. Most of our ideas and thoughts do not surface in the outer world, where they can be realized.

If we don't end up reaching any one of our goals, no matter how "small," we'll lose confidence in our abilities; we'll feel incompetent and even dejected. That's why it's so important to reach our goals, even though at times we might feel like quitting and we no longer feel that initial burning passion. For instance, even though I lost interest in my philosophy studies at some point, I still had to complete my degree. If I didn't, I'd be stuck. I might spend more years floundering in school or end dropping out entirely—and I would be trapped in this life phase instead of continuing to grow and take on new challenges. Regardless of whether our plans and aspirations change along the way, we have to get over our hurdles and finish our projects, so that we can feel accomplished and have self-confidence. (And now I can say that I'm quite proud of my philosophy degree.)

I know it's hard to face reality, especially when it's so much cozier to be lost in our daydreams. But combating our "laziness" is worth the battle. In fact, doing so is crucial to our survival. I know reality can be grueling, like running up a hill. I often see my life as a long-distance race: there are so many times when I want to just give up and drop dead, yet I am compelled to reach the finish line.

This is also probably why I like running so much—it's a metaphor for my life. Being able to run for long periods of time helps build my endurance and makes me feel as if I am moving forward towards something that I believe in. When it seems as if my entire life is falling apart, running is one of the few things that grounds me and reminds me of my strong desire to achieve my goals; that I can finish the race if I put my mind to it. Below are some useful tips that have helped me accomplish my many projects and goals.

Choose *a* goal

The first thing to do is choose a goal. How do you decide which one to choose from? Why not pick that one that's most feasible and has a higher priority? Try to be as realistic as possible and reflect on your capabilities and limitations. Do you think you can reach your goal within a reasonable time frame? Is it the most important thing on your plate? Realize that if you can't choose one goal, you'll end up not choosing any. And if you choose too many goals, you'll be far less efficient.

Create a short-term strategy

The reason why I'm suggesting a short-term strategy is that, as perceivers, long-term goals don't often work in our favor and end up failing, since we're easily excited by new opportunities and may lose interest in our previous endeavors. The upside of this is that we're flexible and adaptable. A short-term strategy could be something like a one-week plan, as opposed to a yearly plan. A good strategy contains a general outline of what you want to accomplish. For instance, when creating a portrait, you start off with the sketch, before filling in the lines with color and shadows.

Break things down into smaller chunks

The most feasible and efficient way is to get things done in chunks. Start with the basics. You don't have to finish everything all at once. Rome wasn't built in a day. If you need to organize your wardrobe, maybe start by taking everything out of your closet and then sort them afterward. At least have a foundation set, so you can make the next step easier. When you break your workload into chunks, you'll feel less overwhelmed.

A great piece of advice that my long-distance running coach used to tell me is to aim for the next landmark (such as a lamp post), instead of thinking about the finish line. Just focus on one small step at a time, and you'll get there. Applying this analogy to other tasks also feels like a workout; it requires a lot of discipline, but the satisfaction that you get in the end is worth it.

If you feel like the finish line is too far out of reach, keep in mind that you're not going to master the rest of your life in one day. Just relax. Master the day. Then just keep doing that every day.

Turn off distractions

Try to turn off distractions such as the internet, social media, and Netflix. Find a way that works best for you. If you find yourself addicted to certain websites, consider downloading a productivity extension such as StayFocusd (or something similar if it's not yet obsolete). Or perhaps go to a library or a café to get some work done. Get rid of unnecessary and unwanted stuff that is cluttering up your space. Free yourself and your mind from any distractions, so that you can focus on what's important.

Celebrate every milestone

Lastly, don't forget to celebrate your "small" wins. Doing so will give you more motivation and confidence in your abilities. You can determine if you've made progress by measuring your success. I like to create a checklist of things to do because it not only helps me stay organized, but completing tasks also makes me feel more accomplished. It's also wise to keep a journal or planner. I find that not only does it help ground me, it's also nice to see my accomplishments and progress over a period of time.

Chapter 16.

A well-rounded INFP

"Happiness is not a matter of intensity but of balance, order, rhythm, and harmony."
– Thomas Merton

As INFPs, we are on a quest to become our most whole and authentic selves. This involves becoming a more well-rounded and functioning human being. Throughout this book, I've already alluded to the various ways in which we can use our functions to our full advantage. In this section, I'll be more explicit by examining the integration of each of our supporting functions, one at a time.

According to Elaine Schallock, an INFP who is well-rounded has achieved a consistent integration of their functional stack in a top-down fashion. By this, she means that the functions are prioritized and used in a dominant-auxiliary-tertiary-inferior sequence. What this looks like for an INFP is using Fi, Ne, Si, and Te in the right order. Sometimes an INFP may feel like jumping the stack, that is, according to Shallock, trying to appease or satisfy the inferior function. I know when I become frustrated and stressed, I often turn to my Extroverted Thinking—trying to be as pragmatic and as critical as possible—only to find out that it backfires, ending in a bigger mess.

Our inferior Te cannot counterbalance our Introverted Feeling because it's also a judging function, and would not supply our Fi with the new information that it craves. Furthermore, since Te is lower in the stack, it's buried within our subconscious, which prevents us from readily accessing and integrating it. This is why we should turn to our auxiliary, Extroverted Intuition first, which counterbalances our Fi quite nicely, as it is a perceiving function and is also more readily accessible.

Integrating Extroverted Intuition (Ne)

Ne opens our world to new possibilities. It complements our Introverted Feeling so that we don't stay in our heads for too long. This saves us from becoming isolated in our thoughts and disconnected from the rest of the world. When we go out and explore, pick up a book, or engage in different conversations and activities, our world becomes a whole lot more exciting! Ne is what helped me discover new career opportunities and opened my eyes to various professional industries and the latest trends. In fact, the reason why many INFPs enjoy going on adventures, traveling, and exploring different cultures is because of Ne. When wielding

Ne, we are more outwardly open, receptive, quirky, and engaging.

We're also extremely creative and artistic when Ne is well integrated with Fi. Our Extroverted Intuition likes to bounce from idea to idea, brainstorming different things. By using Ne to support Fi, we also find more interesting ways to express our personal feelings, whether it's through art, music, or writing. The healthy integration of Ne also makes us become better conversationalists, and compensate for our lack of Extroverted Feeling, enabling us to probe questions to try and understand others. Because of this, INFPs are typically viewed as good listeners as well as facilitators of conversation. Others sense and appreciate that we are genuinely interested in understanding them for who they are as individuals.

However, INFPs also have a love/hate relationship with Ne. When Ne is not so well integrated, it may run wild and lose control. Sometimes, we feel quite scatterbrained because of it; we may find it difficult to deduce firm conclusions, make important life decisions, and become easily distracted, as we find ourselves contemplating too many possibilities. This can also make us feel very uncertain and doubtful of ourselves. For this reason, it took me a while to pick my major at university and find my career focus. After trying out so many things and wearing different hats, I was finally able to arrive at something—once I consulted the various possibilities with my Introverted Feeling. Introverted Feeling can help us make important decisions by being that voice that says, "Out of all of the possibilities, this option is most aligned with my values, and would best serve its purpose." When it comes to an issue that is not centrally important to us, Fi may not be useful in this circumstance, and this is when we turn to Te to help make the most pragmatic decision.

The effective transitioning into Ne often induces a state of flow, in which we are at ease using our Ne to perceive or to create something, becoming one with the activity at hand. This state of flow is a natural feeling that makes us in-tune with the rest of the universe, without interfering or interjecting personal concerns. It also balances our Fi by enabling us to just "let things be." Although Fi allows us to be determined and passionate, our sole reliance on it would be our greatest pitfall. When we become too protective of it, we resist being challenged and this prevents us from growing. This is what our Ne is there for; to help us go with the flow and embrace whatever the universe has to offer.

Integrating Introverted Sensing (Si)

In contrast to the carefree and explorative nature of Extroverted Intuition, our tertiary Si keeps Ne in check, urging us to become more responsible. Introverted sensing is our memory keeper that archives our experiences. It also gives us our strong sense of nostalgia, wisdom, and tradition. The negative aspect of Si, as explained in the second part of this book, occurs when we jump the functional stack, skipping the use of our auxiliary and instead go straight to using Si. When this happens, we find ourselves in a dominant-tertiary loop, where we end up ruminating on past experiences.

I recall feeling impotent and helpless when I thought that I was a victim of my past. I'd blame my lack of self-esteem and unhappiness because of all of the negative experiences that have taken place in my life. This prevented me from letting go and moving forward in life. Sometimes I find myself relying on past experiences or things that I knew about myself in the past, that are no longer helpful. For instance, in high school, I used to excel in mathematics, and it was one of my strongest subjects, but that was no longer the case when I attended university (with the exception of calculus). I barely passed linear algebra, and I felt tortured taking probability and statistics, yet I grudgingly held on to my math minor trying to prove that I still had the knack for that subject. My GPA lowered as a consequence—not that this matters in hindsight.

A healthy integration of Si entails having been explored through the lens of Fi and Ne. We may hold on to family traditions or collect artifacts and toys from the past after we have personalized them and made it our own, interpreting it in a way that resonates with our deepest values.

Introverted Sensing can also help consolidate our dream worlds, bringing our inner exploration to life and vividly recreating detailed experiences. For this reason, many fantasy writers are INFPs, including J.R.R. Tolkien, author of *The Lord of the Rings,* and A. A. Milne who brought us the whimsical world of *Winnie-the-Pooh*. Si can be very helpful in our creative endeavors by bringing our memories to life, whether we're writing a novel, designing a video game, creating artwork, or performing a piece of music.

One of the most valuable things that Si can help bring in is our wisdom. It recalls life lessons so that we would prevent ourselves from repeating past mistakes, and also helps to clarify matters for future direction. We gather wisdom once it has been filtered through our Extroverted Intuition, which picks up various meanings and insights from our experiences, and Introverted Feeling, in which the insight that was picked up by Ne aligns with our core values. The outcome of this occurrence is beautiful, allowing us to develop deep insights that could bring inspiration and healing to this world. Exploring our past through the lens of Fi and Ne can instill greater confidence in who we are and what we care about.

Integrating Extroverted Thinking (Te)

Extroverted Thinking enables us to approach the world in a rational way. It can be used to help us become more assertive, organized, and pragmatic, as well as helping us solve problems that require the use of logic and objective reasoning. However, because it's an inferior function, it lies within our subconscious, and we may find it elusive and difficult to harness. Sometimes I find this elusiveness mystical, and I am drawn to exploring its use by pursuing thinking oriented interests, such as science and math. Because of Te, I also desire to have some order and stability in my life, despite valuing freedom and autonomy.

Since Te is an inferior function, we must be wary of using it consciously. The intentional use of Extroverted Thinking may run the risk of stepping on our Introverted Feeling's toes and then take over completely. It could ultimately trap us, as we do not only direct criticisms outwardly but also direct it towards ourselves, berating ourselves for not living up to our expectations. When used in an unhealthy way, it becomes a defense mechanism to protect our egos, instead of aiding us in achieving our ideals and goals. As mentioned earlier in this book, my Te is often triggered negatively when I find myself in conflict situations, where my values have been threatened. I then become defensive and critical of the person who hurt me. Resolving the issue involves regaining control of my Introverted Feeling, through validating my emotions and finding a healthy way to express them.

A healthy integration of Te occurs in harmony with our Fi. It can be used purposefully once it has gone through the lens of our Fi, Ne, Si, in which our ideals have been explored by Ne and have taken feedback from Si. Used in a healthy way, Te will carry out our ideals to ultimately serve our Introverted Feeling. A time when Extroverted Thinking came to my rescue was when I needed to land a job. Once I had picked a career focus that aligned with my values, after trying out a number of things and then deciding that this option made the most sense for me, it was up to my

Te to help execute my dreams. As Anaïs Nin says, "Our life is composed greatly of dreams…and they must be brought into connection with the action. They must be woven together."

Extroverted Thinking was the executor that made sure that I was applying to places consistently and that I was developing the skillsets that I needed to make myself more fit for that position. Introverted Feeling fuels my Te with motivation, encouraging it to continue to work hard so that I can achieve my goal. Without Fi as my inspiration, I would burn out quickly and find myself in a ditch. That's why it's important that Te is subservient to Fi and not the reverse.

Moving mountains with Introverted Feeling

The reason I believe that INFPs can move mountains is because of our Fi. We are headstrong because of it. When it comes to what we believe in and how we feel deeply inside, nothing gets in our way. Because of our outward gentleness, we do not show our determination. Fi is like the wind: invisible, powerful, and resolute. We can put everything aside and go through extreme circumstances when Fi fuels us. For example, I can play the piano for hours on end or examine every loophole about feminism to further defend that ideology.

Many famous INFPs have left their trace in humanity because they were compelled to make a difference in this world. For instance, Isabel Briggs Myers wanted to help individuals with their self-discovery, so she founded the MBTI personality assessment. Other famous INFPs include Princess Diana, Fred Rogers, John Lennon, Kurt Cobain, Tori Amos, William Shakespeare, Helen Keller, and Susan Cain (author of *Quiet: The Power of Introverts in a World That Can't Stop Talking*).

Because our strong values deeply motivate us, it's essential for us to stay true to ourselves. While you're trying different things and expanding your horizons, never lose sight of who you are and what you believe in.

Pushing boundaries

A great way to become more well-rounded is to challenge ourselves. This involves putting ourselves in different situations that are outside of our comfort zones. As a person who is highly sensitive, reserved, and shy, I needed to learn how to come out of my shell. Doing so often involves engaging with my Extroverted Intuition, to open myself to new activities and to meet all kinds of people. Another challenge for INFPs is to use Extroverted Thinking in moderation, so that it works to our advantage when it comes to dealing with practical matters that involve organizing and planning. It may be a challenge for INFPs to reconcile our Introverted Feeling, which is expressive and subjective, with Extroverted Thinking, which is systematic and objective, but I firmly believe these functions can work hand in hand when they are well integrated. Below are some activities that can help us INFPs to round out our functions:

Join a public speaking club to build social confidence

Introverted Feeling wants to live authentically, create an impact, and to make a positive difference in the world. For us to do so, we need to connect with people. Although we are now able to do so behind our computer screen, thanks to the internet, it's still not quite the same as meeting people in real life. I find that it's hard for me to articulate my thoughts verbally and feel comfortable in unfamiliar social settings, and so I joined Toastmasters, an internationally public speaking organization. It was one of the scariest things that I've done voluntarily, but I have gotten so much out of it and have met many incredible people.

There are Toastmasters locations all around the globe. I've been to various clubs, including the ones from the universities that I've attended, the ones near my home, and even the one in Shanghai, China! The more often I attend a Toastmasters meeting, the more confident I was in participating and speaking in front of a crowd (though I can't say I still don't get the jitters from talking in front of a crowd). Finding different clubs and trying out Toastmasters for the first time required the use of Extroverted Intuition, to help me be receptive to new possibilities from the external world.

Extroverted Thinking is used to help me prepare and organize my speeches. It also enabled me to organize my thoughts so that they can be expressed articulately. Introverted Sensing also comes into play when it came to memorizing my speeches and familiarizing myself with attending these meetings. As a result, I've become more accustomed to speaking in front of people and receiving feedback. This may be difficult for INFPs who are often shy and sensitive to criticism, but I think that we do become better at public-speaking as it becomes a normal part of our lives.

Organize meet-up events with people outside of your social circle

After graduating from university and returning home, I know I had to put myself out there and network to discover my potential. So, I decided to organize meet-up events by inviting everyone in my Facebook network for an afternoon at a board game café. Most of these people are acquaintances and barely knew them, so hosting these events was stepping outside of my comfort zone. After the first event had turned out to be quite a success, I ended up hosting a bunch more, over the summer. I had a lot of fun engaging in conversations with different people. To help us break the ice, I've even created questionnaires using cue cards, asking people about themselves, their hobbies and background.

The great thing about this experience is that it also facilitated the integration of my functional stack in a top-down order. Planning and organizing involved the integration of Te, the party planner. My Ne was the social butterfly that likes to ask interesting questions, in which a lot of the questions came from the memory banks of Si. At the end of the day, the real host of the party was Introverted Feeling, who wanted to have this "party" to live authentically and engage with the real world.

Pay attention to what's happening in the world

I can't help but live in a bubble. I like to read fiction, play music, and daydream about stuff that's not relevant to what's happening elsewhere. However, I also understand that events in the world affect me in some ways. So now I try to stay current by reading articles about the latest trends in business and technology. Doing so also gives me more inspiration for the work that I do. For instance, by learning the latest updates in Google's search algorithm and discovering how Pokémon Go was helping small businesses, I was able to create more relevant content for my agency. I even watched an intro to a business course online, to learn how the economy works.

By trying different things and stepping outside our comfort zones, we can become more well-rounded.

Chapter 17.

Finding my creative muse

*"I have fallen in love with the
imagination. And if you fall in love
with the imagination, you
understand that it is a free spirit. It
will go anywhere, and it can do
anything." – Alice Walker*

The role of creativity in our lives

Creative expression is the lifeblood of an INFP. We
need it to convey our innermost feelings and values
and to also grow as an individual. I can't imagine
what a world looks like without creative expression. I
think it's what makes us human and not robots.
Although, robots are becoming very creative thanks
to artificial intelligence. They can now make beautiful
artwork, cook gourmet dinner, and perhaps soon
they'll be writing novels and blogs! But that's not the

point. Even though robots may be able to do these things, we definitely shouldn't stop finding ways to explore our creativity—or else we'll no longer be human.

Without creativity, we lose a part of our souls. The imagery that comes to mind when I think of humans losing their essence, as a consequence of not tapping into their creative capacity, is Marx's depiction of the worker who is alienated from his work and its product. Workers in an assembly line help build a product in which they have no say over the design and thus have no meaningful connection to it. From their repetitive and uninspiring mindless labor, they become numb—nothing more than a piece of machinery.

Creativity keeps us emotionally healthy. It facilitates freedom of thought, self-expression, and it also helps us develop empathy. I find my creative outlet through reading, writing, music, and even through playing strategic board games and engaging in physical activities such as taking fitness and dance classes. These examples show that creativity can manifest in all mediums. It's a way for the mind to engage in different concepts, use imagination, and come up with its representation of something. For instance, when reading a novel, imagination is used to take you to a different place and setting, but you also look through the lens of a different perspective—from the eyes of the narrator. This is where empathy comes into play.

Empathy is the ability to understand and share feelings of another. Empathy is what connects us to other people, and is essential for social well-being. When we can relate to another person's perspective and their suffering, we can better forgive ourselves and others. We also feel more connected with our humanity in that way. In fact, a study by psychologists David Kidd and Emanuelle Castano, at the New School for Social Research, has shown that reading literary fiction enhances the ability to detect and understand other people's emotions, a crucial skill in navigating complex social relationships. INFPs can be extremely intelligent emotionally, because of our high empathy.

Creativity also helps with our introspection and self-discovery. Having an empathic understanding of other people induces one to reflect critically on one's experiences and values. I've learned so much about myself through my interactions with other people and listening to their experiences.

Therefore, creativity is truly a way to help me stay calm, whole, energized and happy. Although sometimes, I find myself running low on creative juice. This is where the next part comes in.

Finding creative inspiration

Creativity requires spontaneity

Since my childhood, I've liked to explore my creative side using a variety of mediums: from writing stories, to playing the piano, to decorating my room. These things occurred to me quite naturally. However, as I get older, I find myself struggling to come up with new and original ideas. As a content marketer, it's my full-time job to be constantly developing articles and other forms of content for my agency. Even as a personal blogger, I sometimes run dry on ideas and get frustrated.

But when inspiration comes, it usually hits with a BANG! Where does this sudden inspiration come from? If I were to map out my bursts of creativity on a chart, I get these spikes at times in my life when I least expect it—when I'm doing something random and outside of my usual routine. This may include going on a last minute trip, to interacting with new people, or watching random videos on YouTube.

The thing with spontaneity is that it happens unintentionally. Forcing myself to be creative by staring at a blank page breaks the creative chain; so instead, I simply have to live in the moment and not think too hard about things (and let my Ne do its magic). It helps to put myself out there more to seek out new inspiration, such as going to a meet-up event or picking up a random book. Doing so increases my chance of finding that 'aha' moment. Sometimes, creativity comes to me when I'm simply relaxing and being introspective. So when I'm low on creative juice, I use that time to take a break and relax and do something different. Before I know it, the creativity will start kicking in again.

Perfectionism is the death of creativity

A lot of times, when I'm in the process of producing something, such as a piece of writing, I struggle to get my thoughts out, even though I have an idea in mind. This is because I want to make things perfect, which then prevents me from taking action. Maybe I couldn't come up with a proper sentence, or I have multiple trains of thought, and I'm unsure which one is the best. This kind of thinking leads me down a mental block where nothing is coming out, and then I eventually feel drained.

When I was reading *Everybody Writes* by Ann Hadley, one key takeaway from this book was to write the first ugly draft. This involves spilling out whatever inspiration comes to mind without stopping and thinking about grammar and content. Just let things flow. The editing and fine tuning come afterward.

I have the attention span of a goldfish, and I'm learning how to work with it. If I lose interest in a project, I allow myself to give it a break and try something else and revisit it later with fresh eyes. I also find it helpful to break things down into chunks. Sometimes I start in the middle, or the top, or the bottom. It doesn't have to be in any particular order. I also take additional notes as I write while the idea is still fresh; otherwise, I might lose it. And sometimes, because of deadlines, or because I don't have too much time to spare, I have no choice but to keep pumping out content. Sometimes, working under pressure gives me the adrenaline rush that I need to get things done. Although doing this can be helpful, it's probably not good for the long haul.

Be bold and continue to experience new things

What makes something original is that it's taken from a personal experience. Every person has a story and style that's unique to them. Our ideas do not just come out of thin air, even though it may seem this way at times: it's derived from our interactions with the world, combined with our perceptions. And so, it's essential to continue to stay curious and explore new ideas and places, to fuel our imagination.

Chapter 18.

Lessons that I've learned as an INFP

As we near the end of this book, I thought it'd be nice to summarize all the important lessons that I've learned thus far as an INFP. Below are 25 lessons that I've learned.

1. Don't depend on others for your happiness.

2. There's nothing wrong with you. Trust yourself.

3. When you put other people first, you've taught them that you come second.

4. Without darkness, there wouldn't be light.

5. Don't forget to celebrate the "small" wins in life.

6. Not being able to let go will only trap you—

and ultimately, prevent you from living the life that you want.

7. The more you put yourself out there, the more success you'll have.

8. Don't settle for a relationship that won't help you grow.

9. Heal your wounds by connecting with humanity.

10. Anxiety is a product of your imagination and self-doubt.

11. Happiness is a choice and can be found anywhere.

12. Let yourself know that it's okay to have negative emotions—it's all part of the human experience. It helps you learn and grow.

13. Both crying and laughing feels good.

14. Work on self-compassion instead of self-esteem.

15. When one door closes, another one opens.

16. You can't save people; you can only love them.

17. Your gifts are here for a reason.

18. Replenish your soul with sleep, music, nature walks, books, and good conversations.

19. Nothing gold can stay. So be grateful.

20. You don't necessarily need to have an answer to what you'll do for the rest of your life, but that doesn't mean you can't find success along the way.

21. Being hard on yourself is counterproductive.

22. Don't take things personally. People project negative emotions because of their problems.

23. Just let things happen. Let life flow. Don't force it.

24. Not knowing where you'll end up only makes life more interesting.

25. Stay curious.

Chapter 19.

A letter to INFPs who feel misunderstood

> *"People understand me so poorly that they don't even understand my complaint about them not understanding me."*
> *– Soren Kierkegaard*

Dear fellow INFP,

I'm writing this letter to remind you that your gifts and talents are valuable, even though at times you may feel like the world does not appreciate you.

INFPs tend to be wallflowers; we possess a quiet, shy demeanor. However, that's only how we appear on the surface. As an INFP myself, I know that beneath our outer layer of calm burns a passionate inner flame. We have incredible creativity and compassion that are just waiting to be unleashed so that we can make a difference in the world.

Unfortunately, we often feel misunderstood and invisible. Our dominant cognitive function, Introverted Feeling, makes us keep our deeply held values and feelings private. For this reason, we may struggle to articulate the thoughts and feelings that are the most important to us. For instance, we may experience a slew of emotions when we try to make sense of all of the unpleasant incidents that have taken place in our lives. These emotions can make us feel very heavy, and because they are so complex and private, we often cannot share them with others, which only makes us feel more isolated.

When it comes to our relationships, we also look inward. We tend to be great listeners and natural therapists. It brings us great joy to help others unravel their inner core and learn more about who they truly are. For this reason, the INFP personality type is nicknamed the "healer" and "mediator" in the Myers-Briggs system.

However, our light can attract moths, and our warmth can bring parasites. Because we listen and truly care, we get taken advantage of. We may find ourselves in one-sided relationships, becoming someone's emotional dumping ground—they do all the talking while we do all the listening. This makes us feel under-appreciated for the healing that we can bring. If these toxic relationships persist, we may become melancholy and lonely.

As INFPs, we see things differently from other personality types. We have a vivid imagination that sees the world for what it could be. Likewise, our imagination allows us to put ourselves in other people's shoes and see things from their perspective. Unfortunately, most people treat us as if our imagination is a bad thing. We're told that daydreaming is unproductive and childlike. Daydreaming wastes time. This makes us feel alienated and further misunderstood. But the reality is that our detachment from the outer world stems from our desire to discover the truth about ourselves and our world. We're trying to bring meaning and inspiration to our reality.

Although INFPs are healers and dreamers, sometimes the harshness and cruelness of reality drains our energy. When we become stressed, anxious, or frustrated, our shadow manifests through our inferior Extroverted Thinking function. When this happens, we are no longer our compassionate and gentle selves; instead, we become bitter, judgmental, and extremely critical of every error we see.
For example, I can become very critical of others, especially when my core values are threatened. This causes me to feel extreme resentment towards the person who hurt me. I begin to analyze their viewpoint and attempt to prove to them why they're wrong. If matters do not get resolved, the relationship may become damaged beyond repair.

Also, because I have deep feelings that are hidden from the surface, others hurt me without even knowing it. They say or do things that trigger intense negative emotions. For instance, one time I tried to explain to a friend that I was experiencing internal turmoil due to my personal circumstances. Instead of getting the compassionate response I was hoping for, I was called "too sensitive, self-pitying, and ungrateful."

What makes matters worse is that I often don't communicate how I've been affected by the situation. I keep my hurt to myself. This only exacerbates the pain. I have recently discovered that communicating these feelings through writing or finding another creative outlet to express myself helps me clear up these turbulent emotions.

I know that at times, life can be challenging for all of us because the world can be a cruel place. However, I believe that we face obstacles to become stronger. Each time we are challenged, we gain precious wisdom and insight that help us grow and reach our potential. So, if you're feeling defeated, don't give up. Do not let the bitterness of the world steal the beautiful sweetness and love you possess as an INFP. You can be extremely passionate about something, whether that is playing music, creating art, supporting a cause, or learning about the humanities. Believe in yourself and focus on what you love.

The world can be a very exciting place when we open up to it and let go of whatever is holding us back. I think that INFPs are truly extraordinary because we have the inner light of our idealism combined with our strong values. Our inner light motivates us to keep going and to inspire compassion and imagination in everyone we meet.

INFPs are incredibly talented and caring, and we often give ourselves too little credit because we have high expectations for ourselves. And even though other people may not appreciate or understand our deeply held convictions, that does not undermine their value. The world needs us. We might not be in the spotlight, and we usually go about this world quietly, but we are shaping the world in our gentle way.

INFPs have a strong inner compass that helps us navigate through life's ups and downs. So, even though we may appear to be lost, deep down, we're not lost at all. We're simply walking our unique path. INFP, don't let the world deter you. Keep rocking it! You're doing just fine.

Yours truly,

Catherine

Chapter 20.

More INFP-inspired quotes

"The world of reality has its limits; the world of imagination is boundless."
– Jean-Jacques Rousseau

"I know but one freedom, and that is the freedom of the mind."
– Antoine de Saint-Exupery

"Blessed are the weird people: poets, misfits, writers, mystics, painters, troubadours. For they teach us to see the world through different eyes." **– Jacob Nordby**

"People think I'm nuts because I can sit in a room and be happy by myself."– **Tori Amos**

*"Life is a series of natural and spontaneous changes. Don't resist them—that only creates sorrow. Let reality be reality. Let things flow naturally forward in whatever way they like." – **Lao Tzu***

"People say I make strange choices, but they're not strange for me. My sickness is that I'm fascinated by human behavior, by what's underneath the surface, by the worlds inside people."
*– **Johnny Depp***

*"You psychologists focus on what is wrong with people; I want to focus on what is right and what could be right." – **Isabel Briggs-Myers***

*"I sometimes fall into the trap of doing what I think I should be doing rather than what I want to be doing." – **Bjork***

"I must be an emotional archaeologist because I keep looking for the roots of things, particularly the roots of behavior and why I feel certain ways about certain things."
– Fred Rogers

"The planet does not need more 'successful people.' The planet desperately needs more peacemakers, healers, restorers, storytellers, and lovers of all kinds."
– Dalai Lama

"You can't stay in your corner of the forest waiting for others to come to you. You have to go to them sometimes." **– A. A. Milne**

"The whole world is a series of miracles, but we're so used to them we call them ordinary things."
– Hans Christian Andersen

"Every man has his secret sorrows which the world knows not; and often times we call a man cold when he is only sad."
– Henry Wadsworth Longfellow

"To all the other dreamers out there, don't ever stop or let the world's negativity disenchant you or your spirit. If you surround yourself with love and the right people, anything is possible."
– Adam Green

"My heart and my passions are the most beautiful things about me."
– Anonymous

"Be like a tree and let the dead leaves drop." – **Rumi**

"In the depth of winter, I finally learned that there was in me an invincible summer."
– Albert Camus

"Sometimes, in order to follow our moral compass and our hearts, we have to make unpopular decisions or stand up for what we believe in."
– Tabatha Coffey

"Not all those who wander are lost." – **J.R.R. Tolkien**

*"Once you label me you negate me." – **Soren Kierkegaard***

*"The very basic core of man's living spirit is his passion for adventure. The joy of life comes from our encounters with new experiences, and hence there is no greater joy than to have an endlessly changing horizon, for each day to have a new and different sun." – **Chris McCandless***

"Nothing is more important than empathy for another human being's suffering. Nothing. Not a career, not wealth, not intelligence, certainly not status. We have to feel for one another if we're going to survive with dignity."
*– **Audrey Hepburn***

*"You cannot make yourself feel something you do not feel, but you can make yourself do right in spite of your feelings." – **Pearl S.***

"Remember your dreams and fight for them. You must know what you want from life. There is just one thing that makes your dream become impossible: the fear of failure." – **Paulo Coelho**

Conclusion

I've learned so much about myself through discovering the INFP personality type. However, I believe that the things that truly define me are not my characteristics. My cognitive preferences influence the way I see and interact with the world, but in the end, it's the unique experiences, my values, my willpower, and the choices that I've made that have truly shaped who I am today. So hopefully, now that you've finished reading this book, you've gained a deeper understanding of yourself and are inspired to overcome your challenges.

About the author

Catherine Chea is a content marketer and writer based in Toronto, Ontario. She graduated from McGill University with a BA Hon. in philosophy. During her spare time, she enjoys playing the piano and blogging (and frequently writes about being an INFP). Visit her website at www.CatherineChea.com to learn more about her and what she's been up to.

References

Dr. Drenth, A.J. *The 16 Personality Types*. Inquire Books. 2013.

Jung, C.G. *Psychological Types*. New York, NJ: Princeton University Press. 1976. Print.

Kroeger, Otto, and Thuesen, Janet M. *Type Talk: The 16 Personality Types That Determine How We Live, Love, and Work*. New York: Dell Pub., 2002. Print.

Myers, Isabel B., and Myers, Peter B. *Gifts Differing: Understanding Personality Type.* Mountain View, CA: CPP, Inc. 1980. Print.

Ph.D. Berens, Linda. (2013) *Cognitiveprocesses.com: Your Guide to the 8 Jungian Cognitive Processes.* Retrieved from Cognitiveprocesses.com

Quenk, Naomi L. *Was That Really Me?: How Everyday Stress Brings out Our Hidden Personality.* Palo Alto, CA: Davies-Black Pub., 2002. Print.

Made in the USA
Columbia, SC
28 December 2020